Willet Ricketson Haight

Canadian Catalogue of Books

The Annual Canadian Catalogue of Books, 1896

.

Willet Ricketson Haight

Canadian Catalogue of Books
The Annual Canadian Catalogue of Books, 1896

ISBN/EAN: 9783337208790

Printed in Europe, USA, Canada, Australia, Japan

Cover: Foto ©Thomas Meinert / pixelio.de

More available books at **www.hansebooks.com**

1896

THE ANNUAL

CANADIAN CATALOGUE

OF BOOKS

BY W. R. HAIGHT

FIRST SUPPLEMENT

TO THE

CANADIAN CATALOGUE OF BOOKS,

1791-1895.

TORONTO:

HAIGHT & COMPANY,

1898.

TORONTO
PRINTED BY THE CARSWELL CO., LIMITED
22, 30 Adelaide St. East.

NOTICE.

The titles in the Catalogue are given in full, and arranged alphabetically by authors, and, if no author is named, by the first word in the title page. The number of pages follows the title, place of publication, publisher, or printer, year of publication, price and size as per Index Table. When no price is given, the book is published free, or the price was not obtainable.

The Catalogue for 1897 is now in preparation.

LIST OF PUBLISHERS AND PRINTERS.

Anger, W. H. ....Toronto, O.
Banner Printing Company, The................................Chatham, O.
Barthe & Thompson ....Quebec, Q.
Beauchemin & Fils, C. O...Montreal, Q.
Bradley-Garretson Company, Limited, The ....Toronto and Brantford, O.
Briggs, William ....Toronto, O.
Brough Printing Company, The ....Toronto, O.
Brousseau, Léger..Quebec, Q.
Brown & Co., Wm. Foster..Montreal, Q.
Browne, F. N. W..Toronto, O.
Bruce & Co..Toronto, O.
Bryant Press, The ....Toronto, O.
Bureau & Frères, A..Ottawa, O.
Cadieux & Derome ....Montreal, Q.
Cameron, L. K..Toronto, O.
Canada Law Journal Company....................................Toronto, O.
Canada Presbyterian..Toronto, O.
Canadian Advertising Agency ....Toronto, O.
Carrel, Frank ....Quebec, Q.
Carswell Company, Limited, The................................Toronto, O.
Carter, E. S. ....St. John, N.B.
Channell, L. S...Cookshire, Q.
Chatham Planet Book and Job Department ....Chatham, O.
Chénevert, J. A. ....Sorel, Q.
Coombs, John ....Charlottetown, P.E.I.
Copp, Clark Company, Limited, The.............................Toronto, O.
Crain, Rolla L ....Ottawa, O.
Darveau, C...Quebec, Q.
Dawson, Samuel Edward...Ottawa, O.
Demers & Frère, L. J..Quebec, Q.
Drysdale & Co., Wm..Montreal, Q.
Ellis, C. M..Toronto, O.
Era Publishing House, The ....Newmarket, O.
Faveur, Frs. N..Quebec, Q.
Fleming H. Revell Company ....Toronto, O.
Gazette Printing Company ....Montreal, Q.
Goodwin Law Book and Publishing Company, Limited, The ....Toronto, O.
Graham, Hugh..Montreal, Q.
Grandpré, A. de ....Montreal, Q.
Gunn & Co., G. H. ....Chatham, O.
Haight & Company ....Toronto, O.
Hart & Riddell ....Toronto, O.
Hawke, John T..Moncton, N.B.

Hill Printing Company ....Toronto, O.
Hunter, Rose Company, Limited, The...........................Toronto, O.
Imrie, Graham & Company ....Toronto, O.
James & Williams ....Toronto, O.
Jubien, A. E. and R. A. Isner...................................Halifax, N.S.
Langlois, Charles François ....Quebec, Q.
London Printing and Lithographing Company, Limited.............London, O.
Lovell & Son, John ....Montreal, Q.
Massey Press, The..Toronto, O.
Mercier & Cie ....Levis, Q.
Might Directory Company of Toronto, Limited ....Toronto, O.
Monetary Times Printing Company, Limited ....Toronto, O.
Morning Chronicle Office ....Halifax, N.S.
Morning Herald Office ....Halifax, N.S.
Morrow, R. A. H ....St. John, N.B.
Mortimer, C. H...Toronto, O.
Murray Printing Company...Toronto, O.
McLean, R. G..Toronto, O.
McMillan, J. & A..St. John, N.B.
Newton & Treloar ....Toronto, O.
Ontario Publishing Company, Limited, The ....Toronto, O.
Oxford Press ....Toronto, O.
Philip, David ....Winnipeg, M.
Pickwell Bros ....Niagara, O.
Pierre-Georges Roy. ....Levis, Q.
Proulx & Proulx ....Quebec, Q.
Province Publishing Company, The.............................Victoria, B.C.
Pruneau & Kirouac...Quebec, Q.
Railway and Commercial Printing Company, The ....Montreal, Q.
Reid, John A..Regina, N.W.T.
Renouf, E. M. ....Montreal, Q.
Robertson, J. Ross..Toronto, O.
Robinson, C. Blackett ....Toronto, O.
Rose & Sons, G. M..Toronto, O.
Rowsell & Hutchison..Toronto, O.
Spectator Printing and Publishing Company ....Moosomin, N.W.T.
Spectator Printing Company ....Hamilton, O.
Sun Printing Company, Limited, The ....St. John, N.B.
Theoret, C..Montreal, Q.
Thoburn & Co...Ottawa, O.
Tribune Presses...Welland, O.
Tyrrell & Company, William.....................................Toronto, O.
Union Publishing Company ....Ingersoll, O.
Warwick Bros. & Rutter...Toronto, O.
Western Law Times Publishing Company, The ....Winnipeg, M.
Witness Printing House..Montreal, Q.
Wolfenden, Richard ....Victoria, B.C.

CATALOGUE.

ABBOTT.—A Treatise on the Railway Law of Canada. Embracing : Constitutional Law. The Law of Corporations. Railway securities. Eminent domain. Contracts. Common carriers. Negligence. Damages. Master and Servant. Text of Dominion and Provincial Railway Acts, etc. Forms of proceedings in expropriation. By Harry Abbott, Q.C., of the Montreal Bar, Professor of Commercial Law, McGill University. 38+648 pp. Montreal: C. Theoret. 1896. 8.00. 64.

A. B. C.—The A. B. C. Handbook to Halifax, N.S. 64 pp. Halifax : A. E. Jubien and R. A. Isner. 1896. 10. 10.
Contains numerous illustrations.

ACTS.—Acts of the General Assembly of Her Majesty's Province of New Brunswick. Passed in the month of March, 1896. Printed by order of the Legislature. 472+20 pp. Fredericton: 1896. 1.25. 64.

ACTS.—Acts of the Legislature of the Province of Manitoba, passed in the session held in the fifty-ninth year of the reign of Her Majesty Queen Victoria. Being the first session of the ninth Legislature, begun and holden at Winnipeg, on the sixth day of February, and closed by prorogation on the sixteenth day of April, 1896. The Honorable James Colebrooke Patterson, Lieutenant-Governor. Vol. 1. Public Acts. 112 pp.. Vol. 2. Private Acts. 34 pp. Winnipeg, Man.: David Philip. A.D. 1896. 1.15. 61.

ACTS.—Acts of the Parliament of the Dominion of Canada passed in the session held in the fifty-ninth year of the reign of Her Majesty Queen Victoria, being the sixth session of the seventh Parliament begun and holden at Ottawa, on the second day of January, and closed by prorogation on the twenty-third day of April, 1896. His Excellency the Right Honourable Sir John Campbell Hamilton

Gordon, Earl of Aberdeen, Governor-General. Vol. 1. Public
General Acts. 54 pp. Vol. 2. Local and Private Acts. 162 pp.
Ottawa: Samuel Edward Dawson. 1896. 1.00. 70.
>   Contains also Acts of the Parliament of the United Kingdom. 12 pp. **Orders**
>   in Council of the Imperial Government.   10 pp.   Orders of the Governor-General
>   in Council. 54 pp. Contents and Index. 8 pp.

ACTS.—Acts of the Parliament of the Dominion of Canada passed
in the session held in the sixtieth year of the reign of Her Majesty
Queen Victoria, being the first session of the eighth Parliament begun
and holden at Ottawa, on the nineteenth day of August, and closed
by prorogation on the fifth day of October, 1896. His Excellency
the Right Honourable Sir John Campbell Hamilton Gordon, Earl
of Aberdeen, Governor-General. Vol. I. Public General Acts. 56
pp. Vol. II. Local and Private Acts. 60 pp. Ottawa: Samuel
Edward Dawson. 1896. 25. 70.
>   Contains also an Act of the Parliament of the United Kingdom. 4 pp.

ACTS.—The Acts and Proceedings of the Twenty-second General
Assembly of the Presbyterian Church in Canada. Toronto, Ont.,
June 10-18, 1896. 674 pp. Toronto: Press of the Canada Presby-
terian. 1896. 64.
>   Consists of the Minutes and thirty-four Appendices.

ACTS.—The Acts of the General Assembly of Prince Edward
Island. Anno quinquagesimo nono Victoriae reginae. 108 pp.
Charlottetown: John Coombs. 1896. 1.00. 46.

ADAMS.—School-Children's Teeth. Their universally unhealthy
and neglected condition. The only practical remedy: dental public
school inspection and hospitals for the poor. By J. G. Adams,
L.D.S. 88 pp. Toronto, Ont. 1896. 15. 20.

ADRIFT.—Adrift in the Breakers ; or, the present dangers to
religion. 4+268 pp. Montreal: William Drysdale & Co. 1896.
1.25. 28.

AGRICULTURE.—L'Agriculture dans les écoles, en 41 leçons.
Par les Frères de l'Instruction chrétienne. Contenant plus de 120
problèmes sur l'agriculture, près de 200 expériences et plus de 120
gravures intercalées dans le texte. Ouvrage approuvé par le Conseil
de l'Instruction publique. 190 pp. Montréal : C. O. Beauchemin
& Fils. 25. 25.
>   Copyright 1896.

ALDEN.—Making Fate. By Pansy (Mrs. G. R. Alden). Illustrated. 4+396 pp. Toronto: William Briggs. 70. 29.
>   Copyright 1896.

ALMANAC.—The People's Almanac. A compilation of facts and
figures for the consideration of the Electors of Canada. **Prepared**

as a supplement to The Gazette, Montreal. With the compliments of the publishers. 96 pp. 1896. 39.

Paper cover. Contains numerous illustrations.

ALMANAC.—The Star Almanac of Canada. A Cyclopedia of facts and figures relating to The Dominion, with a calendar for 1896. 494 pp. Published with the Montreal Star by Hugh Graham, Montreal. 25. 39.

Paper cover. Contains portraits.

ALMANACH.—L'Almanach du Peuple. Illustré. 1897. Tirage: 55,000. 28e année. 160 pp. C. O. Beauchmin & Fils. Montreal. 5. 16.

Copyright 1896. Paper cover. No title page.

ANDREWS.—Swimming and Life-Saving. By Captain W. D. Andrews, G.C.V., of the Dominion of Canada Life-Saving Service, etc. Second edition. Ten thousand copies. 160 pp. Toronto : William Briggs. 1896. 25. 59.

Contains 100 illustrations. Paper cover.

ANNUAL.—Annual and Encyclopaedia of Useful Information. 1896. 418 pp. Art Publishing Company. 25. 34.

Paper cover. Contains several portraits.

ANNUAL.—Annual and Encyclopaedia of Useful Information. 1897. 416 pp. 25. 34.

Copyright by the Art Publishing Company, 1896. Contains portraits. Board cover, with the title " The Globe Annual and Encyclopædia, Toronto, 1897."

ARETAS.—The Sermon on the Mount and other extracts from the New Testament. A faithful rendering of the original notes, by Aretas. Reprinted by permission from the Irish Theosophist. 30 pp. 1896. 10. 20.

No title page. Paper cover.

ARMOUR.—The Canadian Law Times. Edited by E. Douglas Armour, Q.C., of Osgoode Hall, Barrister-at-Law. Vol. 16. 2+312 pp. Notes of Cases and Index-Digest for 1896. Edited by E. Douglas Armour, and E. B. Brown, of Osgoode Hall, Barrister-at-Law. 12+518 pp. Toronto: The Carswell Co. (Ltd.). 1896. 5.00 year. 49.

ARMSTRONG.—Songs of the New World. By J. Alexander-Armstrong. 74 pp. Toronto: Imrie, Graham & Co. 1896. 27.

Copyright.

ASILE.—L'Asile du Bon-Pasteur de Québec. D'après les annales de cet institut. 410 pp. Québec. L. J. Demers & Frère. 1896. 50.

Contains portrait.

AUDET.—Historique des Journaux d'Ottawa. F. J. Audet. 46 pp. Ottawa: A. Bureau & Frères. 1896. 25. 41.

AUGE.—Le Livre de Musique. Par Claude Augé. 220 gravures. 176 pp. Montréal: C. O. Beauchemin et Fils. 50. 47.

Copyright 1896. Board cover.

BARR.—A Knight of the Nets. By Amelia E. Barr. 6+314 pp. Toronto: William Briggs. 1.00. 28.

Copyright 1896.

BARRISTER-AT-LAW.—Be Your Own Lawyer ; or, Secrets of the Law Office. Giving in concise form the Mercantile or Business Laws of Canada, the technical points and main features of the law, with hundreds of hints, cautions, warnings and suggestions, together with all the important legal and business documents, forming a work of ready-reference for magistrates, professional and business men, landowners, contractors, etc. Lawyers will also find it invaluable as a condensation of most vital legal points. By a Barrister-at-Law. 148 pp. Published by W. H. Anger, B.A. Toronto. 1896. 1.00. 69.

BARTHE.—Drames de la Vie Réelle Roman Canadien. Par G. I. Barthe. 92 pp. J. A. Chênevert. Sorel, P. Q. 1896. 50. 64.

Paper cover. No title page.

BATE.—Gems of Hope. ¹ In memory of the faithful departed. Selected and arranged by Fanny Bate. 2+282 pp. Toronto: William Briggs. 1896. 75. 7.

Contains frontispiece.

BAXTER.—Historical Records of the New Brunswick Regiment, Canadian Artillery. Compiled by Captain John B. M. Baxter (a member of the N. B. Historical Society), and published by the officers of the corps for private distribution. 8+260 pp. St. John, N.B. The Sun Printing Company, Limited. 1896. 43.

Contains numerous illustrations.

BEAUCHAMP.—Almanach Pour Tous, pour l'année 1897. Contenant recettes utiles, notes historiques, etc., etc. Publié par Jos. Beauchamp. 72 pp. Québec. C. Darveau. 15.

Copyright 1896. Contains portrait.

BEAUCHAMP.—La Revue Légale, publication mensuelle de droit, de législation, de critique et de jurisprudence. Redigée par J. J. Beauchamp, B.C.L., C.R., Advocat et Officier Reviseur. Philippe Demers, B.A., LL.D., Advocat Leandre Bélanger, Notaire. Avec le concours de plusieurs collaborateurs. Tome II., N.S. 4+574 pp. Montreal: C. Theoret. 1896. 5.00 year. 34.

BERNARD.—Un Manifeste Libéral. M. L. O. David et le Clergé Canadien. P. Bernard. 228+68 pp. Québec: L. Brousseau. 1896. 36.

Paper cover.

BETHUNE.—The Canadian Entomologist. Volume 28. Edited by the Rev. C. J. S. Bethune, M.A., D.C.L., Port Hope, Ontario. Assisted by Dr. James Fletcher and W. H. Harrington, Ottawa; H. H. Lyman, Montreal, and Rev. T. W. Fyles, South Quebec. 4+320 pp. London, Ont.: The London Printing and Lithographing Company, Limited. 1896. 1.00. 57.

Contains portraits, plates and numerous wood-cuts.

BIBLE.—Bible Illustrations. A series of plates illustrating biblical versions and antiquities, being an appendix to Helps to the Study of the Bible. 40+126 pp. Printed by William Briggs, Toronto, for Henry Frowde, London, Eng. 50. 5.

Copyright 1896.

BOYLE.—Archaeological Report, 1894-95. By David Boyle. Appendix to the Report of the Minister of Education, Ontario. Printed by order of the Legislative Assembly. 80 pp. Toronto: Warwick Bros. & Rutter. 1896. 64.

Contains numerous illustrations.

BOYLE.—The Township of Scarboro', 1796-1896. Edited by David Boyle. Printed for the Executive Committee by William Briggs. 4+302 pp. Toronto. 1896. 1.00 49.

Contains map, portraits and other illustrations.

BRITISH.—The British Empire League in Canada. Its origin constitution and by-laws, including report of special general meeting, held at Ottawa, March 4th, 1896. 22 pp. Toronto: The Carswell Co. (Ltd.). 1896. 50.

BRITTAIN.—Teacher's Manual of Nature Lessons for the common schools. By John Brittain, Instructor in Natural Science in the Provincial Normal School, Fredericton, N.B. New Brunswick School Series. Prescribed by the Board of Education of New Brunswick. 8+116 pp. Saint John, N.B.: J. & A. McMillan. 1896. 50. 33.

Contains illustrations.

[BROWNE (THOS. A.).]—Annual Reports of the Poultry and Pet Stock Associations of the Province of Ontario, 1895. Published by the Ontario Department of Agriculture, Toronto. Printed by order of the Legislative Assembly. 64 pp. Toronto: Warwick Bros. & Rutter. 1896. 70.

Contains illustrations.

BRYMNER.—Report on Canadian Archives. By Douglas Brymner, LL.D., F.R.S.C., Archivist. 1895. (Being an appendix to Report of the Minister of Agriculture.) Printed by order of Parliament. 28+354 pp. Ottawa: S. E. Dawson. 1896. 25. 70.

Contains folding chart.

BUIES.—La Valleé de la Matapédia. Ouvrage historique et descriptif. Arthur Buies. 54 pp. Québec: Léger Brousseau. 1896. 50.

Contains several plates.

BUIES.—Le Saguenay et le bassin du Lac Saint-Jean. Ouvrage historique et descriptif. Arthur Buies. Troisième edition. 420 pp. Québec. Léger Brousseau, Imprimeur-Editeur. 1896. 56

Contains several illustrations.

BULLETIN.—Bulletin des Recherches Historiques. Archéologie —Histoire—Biographie—Bibliographie—Numismatique. Organe de la Société des Etudes Historiques. 2eme volume. 1896. 196 pp. Pierre-Georges Roy, Editeur-Propriétaire. Lévis. 60.

BUSINESS.—Business Hints. 66 pp. With the compliments of Gordon, Mackay & Co. Toronto. 25.

Copyright 1896.

CAMERON.—McGill Obstetric Note Book. By J. C. Cameron, M.D., Prof. of Obstetrics and Diseases of Infancy, McGill University. 76 pp. Record of Children. 84 pp. Montreal: E. M. Renouf. 1896. 1.00. 44.

Contains illustrations and folding record sheets.

CANADA.—Canada a Field for Emigration. Reprint of an Article from The Haddingtonshire Courier of November 6th, 1896. Specially contributed by Mr. E. Hedley Smith, Factor to the Right Honourable A. J. Balfour, M.P., etc. 8 pp. Ottawa: 1896. 50.

CANADA.—Canada Official Postal Guide, comprising the chief regulations of the Post Office, rates of postage and other information, together with an alphabetical list of Post Offices in Canada. Revised and published annually (with quarterly supplements) by authority of the Postmaster-General. January, 1896. 6+212 pp. Ottawa: S. E. Dawson. Paper. 50. Cloth. 60. Yearly subscription. 75. 51.

CANADA.—Canada Public Accounts for the fiscal year ended 30th June, 1896. Printed by order of Parliament. 230 pp. Ottawa: S. E. Dawson. 1896. 15. 70.

CANADIAN.—Canadian Architect and Builder. Vol. 9. 2+210 pp. 1896. C. H. Mortimer, Toronto, Canada. 2.00 per year. 81.

Contains numerous plates and diagrams.

CANADIAN.—Canadian Magazines and Society Papers. A list of Canada's Magazines, Athletic Papers, Ladies' and Society Journals. Circulation and place of publication, and special lists for special classes of advertising, with rates. 48 pp. Toronto: Canadian Advertising Agency. 1.00. 38.

Copyright 1896.

CANADIAN.—The Canadian Almanac, and Miscellaneous Directory, for the year 1897, being the first year after leap year. Containing full and authentic commercial, statistical, astronomical, departmental, ecclesiastical, educational, financial, and general information. The astronomical calculations have been made expressly for this publication at the Magnetic Observatory in Toronto. 352 pp. Toronto: The Copp, Clark Company, Limited. 30. 57.

Copyright 1896. Fiftieth year of publication.

CANADIAN.—The Canadian Pacific. The New Highway to the Orient, across the mountains, prairies and rivers of Canada. 48 pp. 78. *Montreal*

Contains numerous illustrations. Paper cover.

[CARON (ADOLPHE P.).]—Report of the Postmaster-General for the year ended 30th June, 1895. Printed by order of Parliament. 418 pp. Ottawa: S. E. Dawson. 1896. 25. 70.

CASGRAIN.—The Use of Aluminium in Dentistry. New method rendering its use necessary and easy by means of the Automatic Pressure Apparatus by the inventor and patentee Dr. Edmund Casgrain, Surgeon-Dentist, Vice-President Provincial Board of the Dental Association of Quebec. 16+16 pp. Edited by Barthe & Thompson, Quebec. 1896. 1.00. 31.

English and French.

CASSELS.—Ontario Assignments Act, with notes. By R. S. Cassels, of Osgoode Hall, Barrister-at-Law. Second edition. 16+136 pp. Toronto: The Carswell Co. (Ltd.). 1896. 1.00. 9.

CASSIDY.—The British Columbia Reports, being Reports of Cases determined in the Supreme and County Courts and in Admiralty, and on appeal in the full court and divisional court. With a table of the cases argued, a table of the cases cited, and a digest of the principal matters reported under the authority of the Law Society of British Columbia. By Robert Cassidy, Barrister-at-Law. Volume III. 18, 5-644 pp. Volume IV. 20, 7-600, 26 pp. Victoria, B.C. Printed by the Province Publishing Company. 1896. 7.00 in numbers. 62.

[CHAMBERLAIN (T. F.).]—Twenty-eighth Annual Report of the Inspector of Prisons and Public Charities upon the Common Gaols, Prisons and Reformatories of the Province of Ontario, being for the year ending 30th September, 1895. Printed by order of the Legislative Assembly. 10+116 pp. [James Noxon.] Twenty-second Annual Report of the Inspector of Prisons and Public Charities upon the Central Prison of the Province of Ontario, being for the year ending 30th September, 1895. Printed by order of the Legislative Assembly. 36 pp. Toronto: Warwick Bros. & Rutter. 1896. 70.

Paper cover.

CHAMPION.—History of the 10th Royals and of the Royal Grenadiers from the formation of the Regiment until 1896. By Thomas Edward Champion. 280 pp. Toronto: The Hunter, Rose Company, Ltd. 1896. 1.25. 25.
Contains colored frontispiece, many portraits and illustrations.

CHANNELL.—History of Compton County and Sketches of the Eastern Townships, District of St. Francis, and Sherbrooke County. Supplemented with the records of four hundred families. Two hundred illustrations of buildings and leading citizens in the county. Compiled by L. S. Channell. Including biography of the late Hon. John Henry Pope, by Hon. C. H. Mackintosh, Lieutenant-Governor North-West Territories. 296 pp. L. S. Channell, Cookshire, Que. 1896. 4.00. 80.
Contains map of Electoral District of Compton, Que.

CHIMIE.—La Chimie de la Ferme. Manuel du Fermier. No. 1. 224. pp. Lévis: Mercier & Cie. 50. 21.

CHINIQUY.—The Perversion of Dr. Newman to the Church of Rome: in the light of his own explanations, common sense, and the Word of God. By the Rev. C. Chiniquy, D.D. Third edition. 40 pp. Montreal: Witness Printing House. 1896. 57.
England "Catholic." By Martin F. Tupper, printed on third page of cover.

[CHIPMAN (B. W.).]—Nova Scotia. Provincial Government Crop Report. July, 1896. 90 pp. 43.
Paper cover.

[CHIPMAN (B. W.).]—Nova Scotia. Provincial Government Crop Report. November, 1896. 70 pp. 42.

COLPITTS.—Baptism, How? and for Whom? By Rev. W. W. Colpitts. 48 pp. Toronto: William Briggs. 1896. 15. 28.

CONSTITUTION.—Constitution and By-laws of The National Club. Club House, Bay Street. 20 pp. Toronto: Hart & Riddell, Printers. 1896. 8.

COOPER.—The Canadian Magazine of Politics, Science, Art and Literature. Edited by John A. Cooper, B.A., LL.B. Vol. 6. November, 1895, to April, 1896, inclusive. 4+584 pp. Toronto: The Ontario Publishing Co., Ltd. 1896. 2.50 per annum. 71.
Contains numerous illustrations.

COOPER.—The Canadian Magazine of Politics, Science, Art and Literature. Edited by John A. Cooper, B.A., LL.B. Vol. 7. May, 1896, to October, 1896, inclusive. 4+584 pp. Toronto: The Ontario Publishing Co., Ltd. 1896. 2.50 per annum. 71.
Contains numerous illustrations.

COTE.—Political Appointments, Parliaments, and the Judicial Bench in the Dominion of Canada. 1867 to 1895. Edited by N. Omer Coté (of the Department of the Interior, Canada). 12+508 pp. Ottawa: Thoburn & Co. 1896. 4.00. 49.

Supplement, January, 1896, to January, 1897. Pp. 469 to 507.

COTES.—His Honour, and a Lady. By Mrs. Everard Cotes. (Sara Jeannette Duncan.) 4+322 pp. Toronto: G. M. Rose & Sons. 1896. Paper. 60. Cloth. 1.25. 28.

Contains several illustrations,

[COUSE (WM.).]—Annual Report of the Bee-Keepers' Association for the Province of Ontario, 1895. (Published by the Ontario Department of Agriculture, Toronto.) Printed by order of the Legislative Assembly. 8+38 pp. Toronto: Warwick Bros. & Rutter. 1896. 70.

Contains portraits.

CROCKETT.—Cleg Kelly, Arab of the City. His progress and adventures. By S. R. Crockett. 6+388 pp. Toronto: William Briggs. 1.25. 33.

Copyright 1896. Contains several plates.

CRUIKSHANK.—Battle of Fort George. A paper read on March 14th, 1896, by Ernest Cruikshank, Capt. 44th Battalion. "Ducit Armor Patriae." Transaction No. 1, Niagara Historical Society. 28 pp. Niagara: Pickwell Bros. 1896. 43.

Contains an engraving " The Taking of Fort George." No title page.

CRUIKSHANK.—The Documentary History of the Campaign on the Niagara Frontier in 1814. Edited for the Lundy's Lane Historical Society. By Capt. E. Cruikshank. 216 pp. Welland: Printed at the Tribune office. 50. 51.

Paper cover.

CUSTOMS.—Customs, Canada. List of Ports, Outports, and Preventive Stations, January, 1896. 28 pp. 51.

Paper cover. No title page.

CUTHBERT.—Cuthbert's Arithmetic Exercise Book. No. 2. For use in junior second book classes. 72 pp. The Copp, Clark Co., Limited, Toronto. 5. 63.

Copyright 1896.

CUTHBERT.—Cuthbert's Arithmetic Exercise Book. No. 3. For use in senior second book classes. 72 pp. The Copp, Clark Co., Limited, Toronto. 5. 63.

Copyright 1896.

CUTHBERT.—Cuthbert's Arithmetic Exercise Book. No. 4. For use in junior third book classes. 80 pp. The Copp, Clark Co., Limited, Toronto. 5. 67.
Copyright 1896.

CUTHBERT.—Cuthbert's Arithmetic Exercise Book. No. 5. For use in senior third book classes. 80 pp. The Copp, Clark Co., Limited, Toronto. 5. 63.
Copyright 1896.

CUTHBERT.—Cuthbert's Primary Number-Work; and companion to the common-sense arithmetical calculator. By W. N. Cuthbert, Toronto. 10+80 pp. Toronto: The Copp, Clark Company, Limited. 1896. 25. 28.
Contains numerous illustrations.

CUTHBERT.—Exercises in Arithmetic for use in the junior classes of public schools. Part 1. A collection of problems suitable for first, second and third book classes, involving the simple and compound rules, easy fractions, etc., with answers. Second edition. By W. N. Cuthbert, Toronto. 38 pp. Toronto: The Copp, Clark Company, Limited. 1896. 25. 25.

DAWSON.—Geological Survey of Canada. G. M. Dawson, C.M.G., LL.D., F.R.S., Director. Annual Report. (New series.) Volume 7. Reports A, B, C, F, J, M, R, S. 1894. 1244 pp. Ottawa: S. E. Dawson. 1896. 1.50. 62.
" It is accompanied by eleven maps and illustrated by fifteen plates and diagrams, besides a number of figures in the text."

DEBATES.—Debates and Proceedings of the House of Assembly during the Second Session of the Thirty-first Parliament of the Province of Nova Scotia. 1896. Reported by John M. Geldert and William B. Wallace. 6+148 pp. Halifax, N.S.: Printed at the Morning Chronicle Office. 1896. 64.
Paper cover.

DeCELLES.—Les Etats-Unis. Origine—Institutions—Developpement. Par A. D. DeCelles, Conservateur de la Bibliothèque du Parlement fédéral. 16+438 pp. Ottawa. 1896. 2.00. 61.
Contains portraits and illustrations. Paper cover.

DIGEST.—Digest of " Bigelow on Torts." 1889 edition. 32 pp. Toronto: The Brough Printing Company. 1896. 50. 57.

DIRECTORY.—The Union Publishing Company's (of Ingersoll) Farmers' and Business Directory for the Counties of Dufferin, Peel and York. 1896. Vol X. 8+236+230 pp. Issued biennially by the Union Publishing Co., of Ingersoll. 58.

DOWKONTT.—Murdered Millions. By George D. Dowkontt, M.D. With introduction by the Rev. Theodore L. Cuyler, D.D. 88 pp. Toronto: Woman's Missionary Society of the Methodist Church, Canada. 17. 19.

DREW.—The Burning of the Caroline, and other reminiscences of 1837-38. By Rear-Admiral Drew, commander of the Expedition, and Judge Woods. 24 pp. Chatham: The Banner Printing Company. 1896. 51.

Paper cover.

DUGAS.—L'Ouest Canadien. Sa Découverte par le Sieur de la Vérendrye. Son Exploitation par les compagnies de traiteurs jusqa'a l'année 1822. L'Abbé G. Dugas. 414 pp. Montréal: Cadieux & Derome. 1896. 1.00. 45.

Contains maps.

DUNCAN.—Rural Rhymes and the Sheep Thief. By Eric Duncan. 64 pp. Toronto: William Briggs. 1896. 35. 29.

DUNDAS.—Picturesque Dundas. 192 pp. 1896. 2.

"This souvenir is issued in order to put on record in enduring form some of the attractions of a historic Canadian town." Contains 175 plates.

ECOLES.—Ecoles d'Agriculture de la Province de Québec. Programme d'Enseignement théorique et pratique Reglements. Publié par le département de l'Agriculture et de la Colonisation, Québec. Bulletin. 46 pp. Québec: Proulx & Proulx. 1896. 57.

Contains two folding plates.

ELLIS.—Advanced Chemistry for High Schools. By W. S. Ellis, B.A., B.Sc., Collegiate Institute, Kingston. 6+172 pp. Toronto: The Copp, Clark Company, Limited. 1896. 50. 25.

FAIRCHILD.—Rod and Canoe, Rifle and Snowshoe, in Quebec's Adirondacks. By G. M. Fairchild, jr., Editor of Canadian Leaves, etc. 208 pp. Quebec: Printed by Frank Carrel, Daily Telegraph Office. 1896. 50. 22.

Contains numerous illustrations.

FALLS.—Massey's Magazine. Volume 2. July to December, 1896. Edited by Frederick W. Falls. 6+442 pp. Toronto: The Massey Press. 1897. 1.00 year. 65.

Contains numerous illustrations.

FARR.—The Lake Temiscamingue District, Province of Ontario, Canada. A description of its soil, climate, products, area, agricultural capabilities and other resources, together with information pertaining to the sale of public lands. Prepared under the direction of the Commissioner of Crown Lands. By C. C. Farr. 16 pp. Toronto: Warwick Bros. & Rutter. 1896. 70.

Contains map. Paper cover.

FENETY.—Life and Times of the Hon. Joseph Howe (the Great Nova Scotian and Ex-Lieut. Governor). With brief references to some of his prominent contemporaries. By G. E. Fenety. 16+376 pp. St. John, N.B.: E. S. Carter, "Progress" Office. 1896. 1.50. 28.

Contains numerous portraits and illustrations. Errata slip inserted at end of volume.

[FERGUSON (IDA MAY).]—Tisab Ting; or, The Electrical Kiss. By Dyjan Fergus. 300 pp. The Hunter, Rose Co., Ltd. Toronto. 50. 25.

Copyright 1896.

FINANCIAL.—Financial Returns of Department of Mines for twelve months ending September 30, 1895. Legislature of Nova Scotia. Session 1896. 106 pp. 70.

FINANCIAL.—Financial Returns of Expenditure and Revenue of the Province of Nova Scotia for the year ended 30th September, 1895. 4+266 pp. Halifax, N.S. Commissioner of Public Works and Mines, Queen's Printer. 69.

[FITZGERALD (W.).]—Report of the Superintendent of Insurance of the Dominion of Canada for the year ended 31st December, 1895. Printed by order of Parliament. 116+452 pp. Ottawa: S. E. Dawson. 1896. 35. 66.

FITZGIBBON.—A Historic Banner. A paper read on February 8th, 1896. By Mary Agnes Fitzgibbon. Transaction No. 1. Woman's Canadian Historical Society of Toronto. 24 pp. Toronto: William Briggs. 25. 50.

Paper cover.

FLETCHER.—Elementary Greek Prose Composition, with exercises based on Xenophon, Anabasis, B. 1, Ch. 1-8. By J. Fletcher, M.A., LL.D., and A. B. Nicholson, B.A. New edition. 6+180 pp. Toronto: The Copp, Clark Company, Limited. 1896. 1.25. 25.

FOSTER.—Speech on the Manitoba School Question. By Hon. George E. Foster, Minister of Finance. Delivered in the House of Commons, March 13th, 1896. (From Hansard, revised.) 24 pp. 46.

FOSTER.—Commentaries on the Constitution of the United States, Historical and Juridical, with observations upon the ordinary provisions of state constitutions and a comparison with the constitutions of other countries. By Roger Foster, of the New York Bar. Volume 1. 8+714 pp. Boston: The Boston Book Company. Toronto: The Carswell Co., Ltd. 1896. 4.50. 61.

F. T. D.—A New Course of Study in Bookkeeping, with Business Forms. Elementary course, theoretical and practical, for the use of elementary schools. By F. T. D. 120 pp. Levis: Printed by Mercier & Co., Ferry Hill. 30. 51.

F. T. D.—Nouveau Cours de Commerce et de Comptabilité. Cours élémentarie, théorique et pratique a l'usage des écoles élémentaires et des écoles modèles. Par F. T. D. 126 pp. Lévis: Imprimerie Mercier & Cie. Côte du Passage. 30. 51.

GARLAND.—Report of the Loan Companies and Building Societies of the Dominion of Canada for the year 1895. With comparative tables of the chief items for years from 1867 to 1895, inclusive. Prepared by order of the Deputy Minister of Finance. By N. S. Garland, F.S.S., F.S.A., Clerk of Financial Statistics. 20+190 pp. Ottawa: Government Printing Bureau. 1896. 25. 70.

GHYVELDE.—La Bonne Ste. Anne. Sa Vie. Ses Miracles. Ses Sanctuaires. Avec 22 belles gravures hors texte. Par le R. P. Frédéric de Ghyvelde, O.S.F., Commissaire de Terre-Sainte. 10+370 pp. Editeurs, les Directeurs du Collége de Lévis. 1896. 80. 60.

GRANDPRE.—Le Système Métrique Décimal. Conversion de toutes les Mesures Françaises en Mesures Anglaises. Valeur en francs de toutes les monnaies du globe. Par A. de Grandpré. 56 pp. Montréal. A. de Grandpré. 1896. 50. 56.

Contains folding diagram.

GRENIER.—La Science de la Réclame. Par. W. A. Grenier. 4+82 pp. Montréal: The Railway and Commercial Printing Co. 1896. 50. 22.

Contains illustrations. Paper cover.

GRUBB.—Behold Your God! Being seventeen addresses by Rev. G. C. Grub, M.A. Ten Bible readings by Mrs. W. K. Campbell. Addresses to children by Mr. E. C. Millard. Notes of the prayer meetings conducted by Mr. W. K. Campbell, during their mission in the City of Toronto, Canada, February 15th to March 2nd, 1896. 328 pp. Toronto: Reported and published by Bruce & Co. 1896. 75. 57.

Contains portraits.

GUIDE.—Guide du Colon. Province de Québec. Préparé sous la direction de l'Honorable E. J. Flynn, Commissaire des terres de la Couronne. 4+168 pp. 1896. 57.

GUNN.—Gunn's Tested Recipes. A practical, everyday cook book. 32 pp. G. H. Gunn & Co., Chatham. 20.

Copyright 1896. Paper cover.

[GUTHRIE (DON).].—Annual Report of the Inspector of Registry Offices for the year 1895. Printed by order of the Legislative Assembly of Ontario. 36 pp. Toronto: Warwick Bros. & Rutter. 1896. 70.

HAIGHT.—Canadian Catalogue of Books. Part 1. By W. R. Haight. 10+132 pp. Toronto: Haight & Company. 1896. 2.50. 60.

" It will not be claimed that it is by any means a complete Catalogue of Canadian Books, but only 1,000 titles, so arranged as to be easily referred to. The proposed idea is, to continue issuing the parts until (as near as possible) a complete list may be obtained of all the books and pamphlets printed, or published in the Dominion, from the first printed book in 1767 (1765) to the end of 1895, and from this date to issue annual lists for each year, beginning with 1896.

The prices quoted are all taken from Canadian lists, and are the highest given, and, on the whole, may be considered fairly current prices."—PREFACE.

HALDANE.—Is the Sabbath Binding upon the Christian Conscience? By John Haldane. 32 pp. Toronto: Hill Printing Co. 15. 57.

Copyright 1896.

HARDY.—The Canadian Law List, 1896. Edited by H. R. Hardy, Esq., Barrister-at-Law. Published by the Canadian Legal Publishing Company, 6 Quebec Bank Chambers, Toronto. 140 pp. Toronto: The Monetary Times Printing Co., Ltd. 1896. 2.00. 50.

HARKNESS.—Iroquois High School, 1845-1895. A story of fifty years. By Adam Harkness. 162 pp. Toronto : William Briggs. 1.00. 50.

Contains portraits and illustrations. Preface dated January 28th, 1896.

HELPS.—Helps to the Study of the Bible, comprising summaries of the several books, with copious explanatory notes and tables illustrative of Scripture history and the characteristics of Bible lands; embodying the results of the most recent researches, together with a dictionary of proper names, a Biblical index concordance, and a new series of maps. 24+464 pp. Bible Illustrations; a series of plates illustrating biblical versions and antiquities, being an appendix to Helps to the Study of the Bible. 40+126 pp. Printed by William Briggs, Toronto, for Henry Frowde, London, Eng. 60. 5.

Copyright 1896.

HENDERSON.—The Chronicles of Kartdale. Our Jeames. Edited by J. Murdoch Henderson. 344 pp. Montreal: William Drysdale & Co. 1896. 1.25. 29.

Contains frontispiece.

HENTY.—Bonnie Prince Charlie : A Tale of Fontenoy and Culloden. By G. A. Henty. With eight full-page illustrations by Gordon Browne. 384 pp. Glasgow: Blackie & Son, Limited. Toronto: William Briggs. 1.00 28.

Copyright 1896.

HENTY.—By England's Aid; or, The Freeing of the Netherlands. (1585-1604.) By G. A. Henty. With eight page illustrations by Alfred Pearse, and four maps. 384 pp. Glasgow: Blackie & Son, Limited. Toronto: William Briggs. 1.00. 28.

Copyright 1896.

HENTY.—By Pike and Dyke: A Tale of the Rise of the Dutch Republic. By G. A. Henty. With full-page illustrations by Maynard Browne, and four maps. 384 pp. Glasgow: Blackie & Son, Limited. Toronto: William Briggs. 1.00. 29.
Copyright 1896.

HENTY.—By Right of Conquest; or, with Cortez in Mexico. By G. A. Henty. With eight page illustrations by W. S. Stacey, and two maps. 384 pp. Glasgow: Blackie & Son, Limited. Toronto: William Briggs. 1.00. 28.
Copyright 1896.

HENTY.—Captain Bayley's Heir: A Tale of the Gold Fields of California. By G. A. Henty. With eight full-page illustrations by H. M. Paget. 386 pp. Glasgow: Blackie & Son, Limited. Toronto : William Briggs. 1.00. 28.
Copyright 1896.

HENTY.—For Name and Fame: or, Through Afghan Passes. By G. A. Henty. With eight full-page illustrations by Gordon Browne. 352 pp. Glasgow: Blackie & Son, Limited. Toronto: William Briggs. 1.00. 28.
Copyright 1896.

HENTY.—In Freedom's Cause: A Story of Wallace and Bruce. By G. A. Henty. With eight full-page illustrations by Gordon Browne. 392 pp. Glasgow: Blackie & Son, Limited. Toronto : William Briggs. 1.00. 28.
Copyright 1896.

HENTY.—In the Reign of Terror. The Adventures of a Westminster Boy. By G. A Henty. With eight full-page illustrations by J. Schönberg. 352 pp. Glasgow: Blackie & Son, Limited. Toronto: William Briggs. 1.00. 28.
Copyright 1896.

HENTY.—St. George for England: A Tale of Cressy and Poitiers. By G. A. Henty. With eight full-page illustrations by Gordon Browne. 352 pp. Glasgow: Blackie & Son, Limited. Toronto : William Briggs. 1.00. 28.
Copyright 1896.

HENTY.—The Bravest of the Brave; or, with Peterborough in Spain. By G. A. Henty. With eight full-page illustrations by H. M. Paget. 352 pp. Glasgow: Blackie & Son, Limited. Toronto : William Briggs. 1.00. 28.
Copyright 1896.

HENTY.—The Cat of Bubastes; A Tale of Ancient Egypt. By G. A. Henty. With eight full-page illustrations by J. R. Weguelin.

352 pp. Glasgow: Blackie & Son, Limited. Toronto : William Briggs. 1.00. 28.
Copyright 1896.

HENTY.—The Dragon and the Raven; or, The Days of King Alfred. By G. A. Henty. With eight full-page illustrations by C. J. Staniland, R.I. 352 pp. Glasgow: Blackie & Son, Limited. Toronto : William Briggs. 1.00. 28.
Copyright 1896.

HENTY.—The Lion of the North: A Tale of the Times of Gustavus Adolphus and the Wars of Religion. By G. A. Henty. With eight full-page illustrations, by John Schönberg. 382 pp. Glasgow: Blackie & Son, Limited. Toronto: William Briggs. 1.00. 28.
Copyright 1896.

HENTY.—The Young Carthaginian. A Story of the Times of Hannibal. By G. A. Henty. With eight full-page illustrations by C. J. Staniland, R.I. 384 pp. Glasgow. Blackie & Son, Limited. Toronto: William Briggs. 1.00. 28.
Copyright 1896.

HENTY.—True to the Old Flag. A tale of the American War of Independence. By G. A. Henty. With eight full-page illustrations by Gordon Browne, and six maps. 390 pp. Glasgow : Blackie & Son, Limited. Toronto : William Briggs. 1.00. 29.
Copyright 1896.

HENTY.—Under Drake's Flag: A Tale of the Spanish Main. By G. A. Henty. With eight full-page illustrations by Gordon Browne. 368 pp. Glasgow: Blackie & Son, Limited. Toronto: William Briggs. 1.00. 28.
Copyright 1896.

HENTY.—With Clive in India; or, The Beginnings of an Empire. By G. A. Henty. With eight full-page illustrations by Gordon Browne. 382 pp. Glasgow: Blackie & Son, Limited. Toronto : William Briggs. 1.00. 28.
Copyright 1896.

HENTY.—With Lee in Virginia. A Story of the American Civil War. By G. A. Henty. Illustrated by Gordon Browne. 384 pp. Glasgow : Blackie & Son, Limited. Toronto : William Briggs. 1.00. 28.
Copyright 1896.

HENTY.—With Wolfe in Canada; or, The Winning of a Continent. By G. A. Henty. With twelve full-page illustrations by Gordon Browne. 384 pp. Glasgow: Blackie & Son, Limited. Toronto : William Briggs. 1.00. 28.
Copyright 1896.

[HODSON (F. W.).]—Report of the Superintendent of Farmers' Institutes of the Province of Ontario. 1895-6. (Published by the Ontario Department of Agriculture, Toronto.) Printed by order of the Legislative Assembly. 4+248 pp. Toronto: Warwick Bros. & Rutter. 1896. 70.
Contains numerous illustrations.

HOPKINS.—Queen Victoria, Her Life and Reign. A Study of British Monarchical Institutions and the Queen's Personal Career, Foreign Policy, and Imperial Influence. By J. Castell Hopkins. With a preface by the Marquis of Dufferin and Ava, K.P., G.C.B., etc., late Governor-General of Canada and Viceroy of India. 514 pp. The Bradley-Garretson Company, Limited, Toronto and Brantford. 1896. 3.00. 76.
Contains numerous portraits and illustrations.

HOPKINS.—The Canadian Album. Encyclopedic Canada, or the Progress of a Nation in religion, patriotism, business, law, medicine, education and agriculture; containing facts and faces of some of Canada's chief business men, statesmen, farmers, men of the learned professions, and others. With pen and picture sketches of Canadian institutions, industries, and communities. Edited by J. Castell Hopkins. (Editor of vols. 1-4, Rev. Wm. Cochrane, D.D.) Vol. 5. 488+16 pp. The Bradley-Garretson Company, Ltd., Brantford and Toronto, Ontario. 1896. Cloth. 5.00. Leather. 7.00. 77.
Contains numerous portraits.

HOPKINS.—The Sword of Islam; or, Suffering Armenia. Annals of Turkish Power and the Eastern Question. By J. Castell Hopkins. With a preface by Right Reverend A. Sweatman, D.D., D.C.L., Lord Bishop of Toronto. 466 pp. The Bradley-Garretson Co., Ltd., Brantford and Toronto. 1896. 1.75. 32.
Contains numerous illustrations.

HORNER.—Original and Inbred Sin. By Rev. Ralph C. Horner, B.O. 148 pp. Ottawa: Rolla L. Crain, Printer. 1896. 50. 29.

HUGGARD.—The Western Law Times of Canada. Editor: J. T. Huggard, Winnipeg, Barrister-at-Law. Vol. 6. 4+94 pp. Winnipeg, Canada: The Western Law Times Publishing Company. 1896. Times and Reports. 6.00. 50.
Contains the numbers January to November, 1895, inclusive.

HUGGARD.—The Western Law Times Reports. Editor: J. T. Huggard, Winnipeg, Barrister-at-Law. Vol. 6. 16+170 pp. Winnipeg, Canada: The Western Law Times Publishing Company. 1896. Reports and Times. 6.00. 50.

2

HUNT.—Poems and Pastels. By William Edward Hunt (Keppell Strange). 138 pp. Toronto: William Briggs. 1896. 1.00. 28.

HUTTON.—First Steps in Composition. Part I. First and second book classes. By W. A. Hutton, Principal Tilbury Public School, and T. N. Leigh, Principal Tilbury Separate School. 6+100 pp. Toronto: The Copp, Clark Company, Limited. 25. 28.
Copyright 1896.

HUTTON.—First Steps in Composition Exercise Book, No. 1. By Hutton and Leigh. For use in first book classes. 76 pp. The Copp, Clark Company, Limited, Toronto. 10. 68.
Copyright 1896.

HUTTON.—First Steps in Composition Exercise Book, No. 2. By Hutton and Leigh. For use in junior second book classes. 72 pp. The Copp, Clark Company, Limited, Toronto. 10. 72.
Copyright 1896.

HUTTON.—First Steps in Composition Exercise Book, No. 3. By Hutton & Leigh. For use in senior second book classes. 72 pp. The Copp, Clark Company, Limited, Toronto. 10. 67.
Copyright 1896.

HYDE.—A Practical English Grammar for grammar schools, ungraded schools, academies, and the lower grades in high schools. By Mary F. Hyde. Adapted to the use of Canadian schools. By Dr. Fred. W. Kelley, of the Protestant High School, and P. J. Leitch, of the Catholic Commercial Academy, Montreal, Quebec. 8+270 pp. Toronto: The Copp, Clark Company, Limited. 1896. 50. 30.

HYDE.—Practical Lessons in the Use of English. By Mary F. Hyde, formerly Teacher of Composition in the State Normal School, Albany, N.Y. Adapted to the use of Canadian Schools. By Dr. Fred. W. Kelley, of the Protestant High School, and P. J. Leitch, of the Catholic Commercial Academy, Montreal, Que. Authorized for use in the Province of Quebec. 12+160 pp. Toronto: The Copp, Clark Company, Limited. 30. 26.
Copyright 1896. Contains illustrations.

INSTITUTE.—The Institute of Chartered Accountants of Ontario. Incorporated under Act 46 Victoria, chapter 64, of Ontario. Charter of Incorporation, by-laws and curriculum, list of members 1896. 56 pp. Toronto: Monetary Times Printing Company, Ltd. 1896. 25.

INSTRUCTIONS.—Instructions to Assessors in Making the Assessments of Property in the Municipalities of the Province of Ontario Compiled from " The Consolidated Assessment Act," 1892, and Assessment Amendment Acts of 1893, 1894, 1895. 32 pp. Toronto : Hart & Riddell. 1896. 15. 48.

Paper cover.

ISARD.—Wayside Songs. By Mrs. E. A. Isard. 224 pp. Printed for the author by The Era Publishing House, Newmarket. 1896. 1.00. 28.

[JAMES (C. C.).]—Annual Report of the Bureau of Industries for the Province of Ontario, 1895. Parts 1, 2 and 3. Agricultural Statistics. (Published by the Ontario Department of Agriculture.) Printed by order of the Legislative Assembly of Ontario. 8+148 pp. Toronto: Warwick Bros. & Rutter. 1896. 70.

[JOHNSON (GEORGE).]—The Statistical Year-Book of Canada for 1895. Eleventh year of issue. Issued by the Department of Agriculture. 8+1008 pp. Ottawa: Government Printing Bureau. 1896. 46.

Contains folding sheets of tables and map.

[JOLY DE LOTBINIERE (H. G.).]—Report, Returns and Statistics of the Inland Revenues of the Dominion of Canada for the Fiscal year ended 30th June, 1896. Part 1. Excise, etc. Printed by order of Parliament. 34+186 pp. Ottawa: S. E. Dawson. 1896. 15. 70.

JOURNAL.—Journal and Proceedings of the House of Assembly of the Province of Nova Scotia. Session 1896. 1596 pp. Halifax, N.S.: The Commissioner of Public Works and Mines, Queen's Printer. 1896. 64.

Contains folding tables.

JOURNAL.—Journal and Proceedings of the Legislative Council of the Province of Nova Scotia. Session 1896. 1596 pp. Halifax, N.S.: The Commissioner of Public Works and Mines, Queen's Printer. 1896. 64.

Contains folding tables.

JOURNAL.—Journal of the Canadian Bankers' Association. Vol. III., containing October, 1895, to July, 1896. 8+442 pp. Toronto: Monetary Times Printing Company, Limited. 1896. 46.

Contains map and portrait.

JOURNALS.—Journals of the Legislative Assembly of Manitoba. From the 6th day of February to the 16th day of April, A.D. 1896 (both days inclusive.) In the fifty-ninth year of the reign of Our Sovereign Lady Queen Victoria. Being the first session of the ninth Legislature of Manitoba. Session 1896. Printed by order of the Legislative Assembly. Volume 28. 28+112+358 pp. Winnipeg, Man.: David Philip, A.D. 1896. 61.

JOURNALS.—Journals of the Legislative Assembly of the Province of New Brunswick, from the 13th February to the 20th March, 1896; being the first session of the second Legislative Assembly. 1430 pp. Fredericton: 1896. 60.

Contains some views of buildings.

JOURNALS.—Journals of the Legislative Assembly of the Province of Ontario. From 11th February, 1896, to 7th April, 1896 (both days inclusive). In the fifty-ninth year of the reign of Our Sovereign Lady Queen Victoria. Being the second session of the eighth Legislature of Ontario. Session, 1896. Printed by order of the Legislative Assembly. Vol. XXIX. 454 pp. 64.

[KELSO (J. J.).]—Third Report of Work under the Children's Protection Act, Ontario, for the year ending December 31, 1895. Presented by the Superintendent of Neglected and Dependent Children of Ontario. 4+80 pp. Toronto: Warwick Bros. & Rutter. 1896. 70.

Contains plates. Paper cover.

KERNIGHAN.—The Khan's Canticles. By R. K. Kernighan. 240 pp. Hamilton: Spectator Printing Company. 1896. 1.25. 29.

KINGSFORD.—Commentaries on the Law of Ontario. Being Blackstone's Commentaries on the Laws of England adapted to the Province of Ontario. By R. E. Kingsford, M.A., LL.B., formerly one of the Lecturers of the Law Society of Upper Canada. Vol. 1. Rights of Persons. 8+458 pp. Toronto: The Carswell Co. (Ltd.). 1896. 5.00. 49.

KINGSFORD.—Manual of the Law of Landlord and Tenant, for use in the Province of Ontario. By R. E. Kingsford, M.A., LL.B., Barrister, Toronto. 20+252 pp. Toronto: The Carswell Co. (Ltd.). 1896. 1.00. 14.

KINGSLEY.—Stephen, a Soldier of the Cross. By Florence Morse Kingsley. 370 pp. Toronto: William Briggs. 75. 28.

Copyright 1896. Contains portrait.

KINGSTON.—The Circuit Guide. For the especial use of Judges and Lawyers. Spring Assizes, 1896. Containing in concise form different arrangements of the Assize Lists. Besides other useful information of interest to the profession. By George Allan Kingston, of Osgoode Hall, Barrister-at-Law. 60 pp. Toronto: The Bryant Press. 1896. 25. 4.

Errata slip inserted.

KINGSTON.—The Circuit Guide. For the especial use of Judges and Lawyers. Autumn Assizes, 1896. Containing in concise form different arrangements of the Assize Lists. Besides other useful information of interest to the profession. By George Allan Kingston, of Osgoode Hall, Barrister-at-Law. 60 pp. Toronto: The Bryant Press. 1896. 25. 6.

KIRBY.—Annals of Niagara. By William Kirby, F.R.S.C. 270 pp. Tribune Presses, Welland, Ontario. 1896. Paper. 75. Cloth. 1.00. 57.

KIRK.—Part of the Trail Creek Mining Camp, West Kootenay, British Columbia. April, 1897. Compiled by the undersigned, J. A. Kirk, Provincial Land Surveyor, Rossland, B.C. Size of map, 37x34. 2.00. 83.
Colored folding map in cloth case. Copyright 1896.

LAMBE.—Hand-book. Duties and Successions in Province of Quebec, with text of statutes in English and French, and forms of declarations. By Wm. B. Lambe, Advocate. 70 pp. Montreal: Wm. Foster Brown & Co. 1896. 50. 57.

LANG.—Elementary Composition Exercise Book, No. 1. By S. E. Lang, B.A., Inspector of Schools, Northwestern Division, Manitoba. For use in second book classes. Exercises on the paragraph. Part 1, Exercises in unity; Finding and classifying material. Part 2, Exercises in arrangement of narrative. 60 pp. The Copp, Clark Company, Limited, Toronto. 10. 68.
Copyright 1896.

LaROQUE.—Manuel des Engrais. Par le Dr. G. LaRoque de Québec. 242 pp. Lévis: Mercier & Cie. 35. 24.
Copyright 1896. Contains eight woodcuts.

[LAROUSSE].—Nouveau Dictionnaire Illustré Historique, Géographique, Biographique et Mythologique, comprenant environ 5,000 articles concernant le Canada. Nouvelle édition (15e). Revue et corrigée avec soin, considérablement augmentée et contenant 260 portraits des personnages les plus célèbres du Canada et de l'étranger. 4+304 pp. Montréal: C. O. Beauchemin & Fils. 1896. 75. 12.

LESLIE.—Rhymes of the Kings and Queens of England. By Mary Leslie. Being an account of the Rulers of England from the Norman Conquest to the reign of Victoria. With numerous illustrations. 178 pp. Toronto: William Briggs. 1896. 1.00. 28.

LIVRE.—Livre de Lecture Courante. Par les Frères du Sacre-Coeur. Cours élémentaire. 164 pp. Lévis: Mercier & Cie. 20. 24.
Copyright 1896. Contains numerous illustrations.

LIZARS.—In the days of the Canada Company: The Story of the Settlement of the Huron Tract and a view of the social life of the period. 1825-1850. By Robina and Kathleen Macfarlane Lizars. With an introduction by G. M. Grant, D.D., LL.D., Principal

Queen's University, Kingston. With portraits and illustrations. 494 pp. Toronto: William Briggs. 1896. 2.00. 50.

LORIMIER.—La Revue de Jurisprudence, ou recueil de decisions des divers tribunaux de la Province de Québec, par une réunion de juges et de jurisconsultes sous la direction de Charles Chamilly de Lorimier, Juge de la Cour Supérieure pour la Province de Québec. 10+620 pp. Montréal: C. Theoret. 5.00 year. 34.

Volume 2, 1896.

MACADAM.—The Master's Memorial. A Manual on the Lord's Supper. For class and private study. By the Rev. Thomas Macadam, late Professor of Mental and Moral Philosophy and Systematic Theology, Morrin College, Quebec. Fifth edition. 40 pp. Montreal: W. Drysdale & Co. 1896. 10. 16.

MACDONELL.—The Ontario Boundary Controversy: Legal and Constitutional, Political and Historical: The Proceedings before the Imperial Privy Council, with selections from the documents in evidence, a special appendix, and an elaborate illustrative historical map. Edited with critical and explanatory notes, by John P. Macdonell, of the Ontario Civil Service. 6+422 pp. Toronto: The Carswell Company. 1896. 1.00. 70.

MACKENZIE.—The Six Nations Indians in Canada. By J. B. Mackenzie. 2+152 pp. The Hunter, Rose Company, Ltd., Toronto. 1.00. 26.

Copyright 1896.

MACKENZIE.—Trinity College Year Book, 1895-1896. Published by order of the Executive Committee of Convocation, and edited by Michael Alexander Mackenzie, M.A., Professor of Mathematics and Physics, and Archibald Hope Young, M.A., Lecturer in Modern Languages and Philology. 8+182 pp. Toronto: Oxford Press. 50. 35.

Contains portraits and illustrations.   Paper cover.   Preface dated November 14th, 1896.

MACLAREN.—Banks and Banking. The Bank Act, Canada : with notes, authorities and decisions, and the Law relating to warehouse receipts, bills of lading, etc. Also the Savings Bank Act, the Winding Up Act, and extracts from the Criminal Code, 1892. By J. J. Maclaren, Q.C., D.C.L., LL.D., Member of the Bar of Ontario and of Quebec. With an introduction on Banking in Canada. By B. E. Walker, Esq., General Manager of the Canadian Bank of Commerce. 58+326 pp. Toronto : The Carswell Co., Ltd. 1896. 4.50. 49.

MACLAREN.—Bills, Notes and Cheques. The Bills of Exchange Act, 1890, Canada, and amending Acts, with notes and illustrations from Canadian, English and American decisions, and references to ancient and modern French Law. By J. J. Maclaren, Q.C., D.C.L., LL.D., Member of the Bar of Ontario and of Quebec. Second edition. 60+546 pp. Toronto: The Carswell Co., Ltd. 1896. 5.50. 50.

MACLEAN.—Canadian Savage Folk. The Native Tribes of Canada. By John Maclean, M.A., Ph.D., Member of the American Society for the Advancement of Science, etc. Illustrated. 642 pp. Toronto: William Briggs. 1896. 2.50. 50.

MACLEAN.—The Warden of the Plains, and other Stories of Life in the Canadian North-West. By John Maclean, M.A., Ph.D. Illustrated by J. E. Laughlin. 302 pp. Toronto: William Briggs. 1896. 1.25. 32.

MASSEY.—Hart Almerrin Massey; Pioneer farmer, farm implement manufacturer, public-spirited citizen, philanthropist. Died at his residence in Toronto, Canada, Thursday evening, February 20th, 1896. 70 pp. 52.
Contains portrait. Lithographed cover. Printed on one side of leaf only.

MASSEY.—Massey's Magazine. Volume 1. January to June, 1896. 8+434 pp. Toronto: The Massey Press. 1896. 1.00 year. 65.
Contains numerous illustrations.

MASSICOTTE.—Le Droit Civil Canadien, résumé en tableaux synoptiques. D'après la méthode de A. Wilhelm. Par E. Z. Massicotte, LL.B., Avocat, Montreal. 4+128 pp. Montreal: C. Theoret, Editeur, 1896. 1.00. 70.

MATHIEU.—Rapports Judiciaires Revisés de la Province de Québec comprenant la revision complète et annotée de toutes les causes rapportées dans les différentes revues de droit de cette Province jusqu'au 1er Janvier, 1892. Ainsi que des causes jugées par la Cour Suprême et le Conseil Privé sur appel de nos tribunaux. Par l'Honorable M. Mathieu, Juge de la Cour Supérieure de Montréal. Tome XVI., 8+544 pp.; XVII., 8+578 pp.; XVIII., 10+594 pp. Montréal: C. O. Beauchemin & Fils. 1896. 7.00 per volume. 58.
Sold to subscribers to the entire work only.

MEAT.—On Meat and Milk Inspection. Containing the Act providing for the inspection of meat and milk supplies of cities and towns; plans and estimate of cost of a municipal abattoir, and regulations of the Provincial Board of Health regarding the same; also report on inspection of meat and milk and regulations relating thereto. Issued by Provincial Board of Health of Ontario. 34 pp. Toronto: Warwick Bros. & Rutter. 1896. 57.
Pamphlet No. 1, 1896.

MERCHANT.—High School Physical Science. Part 2. By F. W. Merchant, M.A., Collegiate Institute, London. Authorized by the

Department of Education for Ontario. 6+446 pp. Toronto: The Copp, Clark Company, Limited. 1896. 75. 25.

Contains 281 illustrations.

[MIALL (E.).]—Report, Returns and Statistics of the Inland Revenues of the Dominion of Canada for the fiscal year ended 30th June, 1896. Part 2. Inspection of Weights and Measures, Gas and Electric Light. Printed by order of Parliament. 6+60 pp. Ottawa. S. E. Dawson. 1896. 10. 70.

[MIALL (EDWARD).]—Report, Returns and Statistics of the Inland Revenues of the Dominion of Canada for the fiscal year ended 30th June, 1896. Part 3. Adulteration of Food. Printed by order of Parliament. 6+156 pp. Ottawa: S. E. Dawson. 1896. 10. 74.

MILLAR.—School Management and the Principles and Practice of Teaching. With an appendix containing the statutory provisions of 1896, relating to continuation classes, duties of teachers, agreements, etc., and the courses of study for high and public schools. By John Millar, B.A., Deputy Minister of Education for Ontario. 292 pp. Toronto: William Briggs. 1896. 1.00. 24.

MILLER.—The Students' History Note Book. By Rev. J. O. Miller, M.A., Principal of Ridley College, St. Catharines. 114 pp. Toronto: The Copp, Clark Company, Limited. 25. 53.

Copyright 1896. Contains maps and colored diagrams.

MOCKRIDGE.—The Bishops of the Church of England in Canada and Newfoundland, being an illustrated historical sketch of the Church of England in Canada, as traced through her Episcopate. By Rev. Charles H. Mockridge, M.A., D.D., Canon of St. Alban's Cathedral, Toronto, etc. 12+380 pp. Toronto: F. N. W. Browne. 3.00. 51.

Copyright 1896. Contains numerous portraits and illustrations.

MONTIZAMBERT.—Annual Report of the General Superintendent of Canadian Quarantines. F. Montizambert, M.D., F.R.C.S., D.C.L. 18 pp. 70.

Report dated 31st October, 1896.

MOORE.—Culture des Fruits dans la Province de Québec et plus particulièrement dans la partie est de la Province. Par George Moore. Bulletin No. 3 du Département de l'Agriculture et de la Colonisation. Deuxième édition, revue et augmentée par M. J. C. Chapais, Assistant-Commissaire de l'industrie laitière, et M. Auguste Depuis, horticulteur. 60 pp. Québec. Charles François Langlois. 1896. 71.

Contains folding table. Paper cover.

MULOCK.—Speech. By Mr. Mulock at Massey Hall, Toronto, on 22nd of February, 1896, on " Remedial Legislation." 8 pp. 57.

MURPHY.—Report on the Subsidized Railways and other Public Works in the Province of Nova Scotia, for the year ending September 30, 1895. By Martin Murphy, D.Sc., Provincial Engineer, N.S. Published by order. 112 pp. Halifax, N.S.: Commissioner of Public Works and Mines, Queen's Printer. 1896. 73.

[MacCALLUM (G. A.).]—Report of the Ontario Game and Fish Commissioners for the year 1895. Printed by the order of the Legislative Assembly. 46 pp. Toronto: Warwick Bros. & Rutter. 1896. 71.

Paper cover.

McCAUL.—Ready Reference Guide to the Ordinances of the North-West Territories. Including the revised ordinances of 1888 and all subsequent ordinances to 1895 (inclusive) together with a complete index to "The Judicature Ordinance" (1893), and amendments thereto. Compiled by C. C. McCaul, B.A., one of Her Majesty's Counsel, and Horace Harvey, B.A., LL.B., both of Osgoode Hall and the North-West Territories, Barristers and Advocates. 6+54 pp. Toronto: The Goodwin Law Book and Publishing Company (Limited). 1896. 1.00. 57.

McDOUGALL.—Saddle, Sled anl Snowshoe: Pioneering on the Saskatchewan in the Sixties. By John McDougall. With illustrations by J. E. Laughlin. 282 pp. Toronto: William Briggs. 1896. 1.00. 28.

McINTYRE.—Le Voyage autour de ma Chambre and le Lepreux de la Cité d'Aoste of Xavier de Maistre. La Grammaire and La Lettre Chargée of Eugène Labiche. Edited with introductions, notes, and vocabulary. By E. J. McIntyre, B.A., Modern Language Master, St. Catharines Collegiate Institute, and F. H. Sykes, M.A., Ph. D., Professor in the Western University of London, Ont. 14+346 pp. Toronto: The Copp, Clark Company, Limited. 1896. 1.25. 25.

Contains portrait.

McKENZIE.—Heartsease Hymns and other verses. By William P. McKenzie. 48 pp. William Tyrrell & Co., Toronto, Canada. 1896. 25. 27.

Paper cover.

MacLEAN.—Appendix to High School Book-Keeping, containing eight short complete sets for beginners, three series of six sets for advanced students, illustrating single and double entry methods, also practical business forms of book-keeping. By H. S. MacLean, Assistant Principal Manitoba Normal School. 212-300 pp. Toronto: The Copp, Clark Company, Limited. 20. 38.

Copyright 1896.

McLEOD.—Geometrical Drawing for the use of Schools and Colleges. By C. H. McLeod, Ma. E., Professor in the Faculty of Applied Science, McGill University, Montreal. 28 pp. Foster, Brown & Co., Montreal. 35. 40.

Copyright 1896. Paper cover. No title page. Contains numerous diagrams. Dominion series of drawing books.

McNAUGHTON.—Overland to Cariboo. An eventful journey of Canadian pioneers to the gold-fields of British Columbia in 1862. By Margaret McNaughton, wife of one of the pioneers. With portraits and illustrations. 176 pp. Toronto: William Briggs. 1896. 1.00. 28.

NOUVELLE.—Nouvelle Lyre Canadienne. Recueil de Chansons, Canadiennes et Françaises. Nouvelle édition, entièrement refondue et considérablement augmentée. 4+456 pp. Montréal: C. O. Beauchemin & Fils. 1896. 30. 11.

O'BRIEN.—The Canada Law Journal. Henry O'Brien, Editor. Vol. XXXII. From January to December, 1896. 12+820+16 pp. Toronto: Canada Law Journal Company. 5.00 year. 64.

[OGDEN (ANNIE L.).]—Cycle of Prayer of the General Missionary Society, the Woman's Missionary Society, Epworth Leagues and Sunday Schools of the Methodist Church, Canada. Copied largely from the Cycle of Prayer of the Student Volunteer Movement for Foreign Missions. 16 pp. Toronto. 3. 82.

Copyright 1896. Paper cover.

ORDINANCES.—Ordinances of the North-West Territories passed in the Second Session of the Third Legislative Assembly, begun and holden at Regina on the twenty-ninth day of September, and closed on the thirteenth day of October, 1896. His Honour Charles Herbert Mackintosh, Lieutenant-Governor. 210 pp. Regina, N.W.T. Printed by John A. Reid. 1896. 1.00. 51.

PAPERS.—Papers relating to the application of the Senate of the University of Toronto to the Universities of Oxford and Cambridge for the grant of special affiliation privileges to the University of Toronto. Printed by the order of the Legislative Assembly of Ontario. 24 pp. Toronto: Warwick Bros. & Rutter. 1896. 70.

PARKER.—The Seats of the Mighty. Being the memoirs of Captain Robert Moray, sometime an officer in the Virginia Regiment and afterwards of Amherst's Regiment. By Gilbert Parker. 10+376 pp. Toronto: The Copp, Clark Company. 1896. Paper. 75. Cloth. 1.50. 28.

PIONEER.—The Pioneer Farm and the Wabigoon Country, Rainy River District. A new section opened for settlement—information as to the country and its capabilities—an account of the farm

established there by the Ontario Government. Published by the Ontario Department of Agriculture. 8 pp. Toronto: Warwick Bros. & Rutter. 1896. 57.
Contains map and plates. Paper cover.

[PLANTE (J. B.).]—Cultures Fourragères, Paturages et Pelouses. 190+6 pp. Mercier & Cie. Lévis. 35. 16.
Copyright 1896.

POLITICAL.—Political Pointers for the Campaign of 1896. "Canada for the Canadians." 52 pp. Ottawa: Printed by Thoburn & Co. 65.

POWER.—The Great Commission. Sermon 1. Mark xvi. 15, 16. The Controversy ended: Immersion not Essential to a Valid Baptism. Sermon II. Peter and the Keys: What they were and what he did with them. Matt. xvi. 19. By Mr. George Power. 32 pp. Toronto: Printed for the author by William Briggs. 1896. 15. 28.

PROCEEDINGS.—Proceedings and Transactions of the Royal Society of Canada. Second series—Volume 2. Meeting of May, 1896. 126+50+6+168+288+180+192 pp. Printed by the Gazette Printing Co., Montreal. 73.
Contains illustrations, plans and diagrams.

RAPPORT.—Deuxième Rapport Annuel du Conseil d'Hygiène de la Province de Québec. Pour l'année finissant le 30 Juin, 1896. 266 pp. Québec: Charles-François Langlois. 1896. 71.
Paper cover. Contains illustrations. Errata inserted after page 46.

READ.—The Canadian Rebellion of 1837. By D. B. Read, Q.C. 14+374 pp. Toronto: C. Blackett Robinson. 1896. 2.00. 42.
Contains portraits.

REPORT.—Annual Report of the Commissioner of Crown Lands of the Province of Nova Scotia, for the year ending 30th September, 1895. 8 pp. Halifax, N.S.: Commissioner of Public Works and Mines, Queen's Printer. 1896. 73.

REPORT.—Annual Report of the Government Inspector upon the Public Institutions of Manitoba, including the Annual Reports of the Superintendents of the Asylum for the Insane, Selkirk; Asylum for the Insane, Brandon; Home for Incurables, Portage la Prairie; Deaf and Dumb Institute, Winnipeg; General Hospital, Winnipeg; St. Boniface Hospital; General Hospital, Brandon; Morden Hospital; Children's Home, Fort Rouge; Children's Home, St. Boniface; Home for Aged Women, St. Boniface; the Women's Home, Winnipeg; the Gaols of Eastern, Central and Western Judicial Districts and the land titles offices. For the year 1896. 98 pp. David Philip. Winnipeg. 1896. 70.
Paper cover. Contains portrait.

REPORT.—Annual Report of the Secretary for Agriculture, Nova Scotia, for the year 1895. 8+208 pp. Halifax, N.S.: Commissioner of Public Works and Mines, Queen's Printer. 70.
Contains a folding table.

REPORT.—Annual Report of the Superintendent of Education on the Public Schools of Nova Scotia, for the year ended 31st July, 1895. 44+152 pp. Halifax, N.S.: Commissioner of Public Works and Mines, Queen's Printer. 1896. 70.
Contains two plates.

REPORT.—Fifth Annual Report of the Children's Aid Society of Toronto. September, 1896. 64 pp. R. G. McLean. 1896. 57.
Contains numerous illustrations.

REPORT.—Forty-first Annual Report of the Chief Commissioner of Public Works, New Brunswick, 1895. Laid before the Legislature by order of His Honor the Lieutenant-Governor. 112 pp. Fredericton, N.B.: Printed by John T. Hawke, Moncton. 1896. 65.
Paper cover.

REPORT.—General Report of the Commissioner of Public Works of the Province of Quebec, 1896. Printed by order of the Legislature. 6+148 pp. Quebec: Charles François Langlois. 1896. 71.
Contains two diagrams.

REPORT.—Official Report of the Debates and Proceedings of the Legislative Council, during the Second Session of the Thirty-first Parliament of the Province of Nova Scotia, 1896. B. Russell, Official Reporter. 56+4 pp. Halifax, N.S.: Printed at the Morning Herald Office. 1896. 59.

REPORT.—Report of the Commissioner of Agriculture and Coloni-zation of the Province of Quebec, 1896. Comprising the subjects relating to Agriculture, the Reports of the Dairymen's Association and of the Pomological and Fruit Growing Society. 210+312+192 pp. Quebec: Charles François Langlois. 70.
Three separate reports bound in one volume. Contains illustrations and folding tables. Paper cover.

REPORT.—Report of the Commissioner of Crown Lands of the Province of Ontario for the year 1895. Printed by order of the Legislative Assembly. 14+104 pp. Toronto: Warwick Bros. & Rutter. 1896. 70.
Paper cover.

REPORT.—Report of the Commissioner of Public Works for the Province of Ontario for the year ending 31st December, 1895. Printed by order of the Legislative Assembly. 42 pp. Toronto: Warwick Bros. & Rutter. 1896. 70.
Paper cover.

REPORT.—Report of the Department of Mines, Nova Scotia, for the year ending September 30, 1895. 4+88 pp. Halifax, N.S.: Commissioner of Public Works and Mines, Queen's Printer. 1896. 70.

REPORT.—Report of the Honorable the Provincial Treasurer on the working of the Tavern and Shop Licenses Acts for the year 1895. Printed by order of the Legislative Assembly. 108 pp. Toronto: Warwick Bros. & Rutter. 1896. 65.

REPORT.—Second Annual Report of the Board of Health of the Province of Quebec. For the year ending June 30th, 1896. (Translation.) 266 pp. Quebec: Charles-François Langlois. 1896. 71.
Paper cover. Contains illustrations. Errata inserted after page 82.

REPORT.—Tenth Annual Report of the Commissioners for the Queen Victoria Niagara Falls Park, 1895. Printed by order of the Legislative Assembly. 80 pp. Toronto: Warwick Bros. & Rutter, Printers. 1896. 70.
Contains a map of the Niagara River, and numerous plates.

REPORT.—Twenty-eighth Annual Report of the Inspector of Prisons and Public Charities upon the Common Gaols, Prisons and Reformatories of the Province of Ontario, being for the year ending 30th September, 1895. Printed by order of the Legislative Assembly. 126 pp. Toronto: Warwick Bros. & Rutter. 1896. 65.
Paper cover.

REPORT.—Twenty-first Annual Report of the Ontario Agricultural College and Experimental Farm. Seventeenth Annual Report of the Agricultural and Experimental Union 1895. (Published by the Ontario Department of Agriculture, Toronto.) Printed by order of the Legislative Assembly. 24+436 pp. Toronto: Warwick Bros. & Rutter. 1896. 70.
Contains numerous illustrations.

REPORT.—Twenty-second Annual Report of the Inspector of Prisons and Public Charities upon the Central Prison of the Province of Ontario, being for the year ending 30th September, 1895. Printed by order of the Legislative Assembly. 36 pp. Toronto: Warwick Bros. & Rutter. 1896. 65.
Paper cover.

REPORTS.—Annual Reports of the Dairymen and Creameries' Associations of the Province of Ontario, 1895. Dairymens' Association of Eastern Ontario. Dairymens' Association of Western Ontario. Creameries' Association of Ontario. (Published by the Ontario Department of Agriculture, Toronto.) Printed by order of the Legislative Assembly. 4+272 pp. Toronto: Warwick Bros. & Rutter. 1896. 70.

REPORTS.—Annual Reports of the Live Stock Associations of the Province of Ontario, 1895-6. Dominion Cattle Breeders' Association. Dominion Swine Breeders' Association. Dominion Sheep Breeders' Association. Dominion Shorthorn Breeders' Association. Dominion Ayrshire Breeders' Association. Hackney Horse Society. Clydesdale Horse Association. Shire Horse Association. Canadian Horse Breeders' Association. (Published by the Ontario Department of Agriculture, Toronto.) Printed by order of the Legislative Assembly of Ontario. 4+168 pp. Toronto: Warwick Bros. & Rutter. 1896. 70.

Contains illustrations.

REVIEW.—The Dominion Review. A Monthly Record of Events and Opinions in Politics, Religion and Science. Vol. I. March to December, 1896. 4+408 pp. Toronto, Can.: C. M. Ellis. 50.

RINFRET.—Dictionnaire de Nos Fautes contre la Langue Française. Par Raoul Rinfret. Quatrieme mille. 8+306 pp. Montréal: C. O. Beauchemin & Fils., Libraries—Imprimeurs. 60. 23.

Copyright 1896.

ROBERTS.—Around the Camp-fire. By Charles G. D. Roberts, M.A., F.R.S.C. Illustrated by Charles Copeland. 4+350 pp. Toronto: William Briggs. 1.25. 32.

Copyright 1896.

ROBERTSON.—Robertson's Landmarks of Toronto. A collection of Historical Sketches of the old Town of York from 1792 until 1833, and of Toronto from 1834 to 1895, also nearly two hundred engravings of old houses, familiar faces and historic places, with maps and schedules connected with the local history of York and Toronto. Republished from the "Toronto Evening Telegram." 16, 564-1128 pp. Toronto: J. Ross Robertson. 1896. Edition, 1,000. 2.00. 57.

Second volume of the "Landmarks of Toronto."

ROBERTSON.—High School History of Greece and Rome. By W. J. Robertson, B.A., LL.B., and John Henderson, M.A. Authorized by the Education Department of Ontario. 8+530 pp. Toronto: The Copp, Clark Company, Limited. 1896. 75. 25.

Contains several colored maps.

ROBERTSON.—The High School Algebra. Part I. By W. J. Robertson, B.A., LL.B., Mathematical Master, Collegiate Institute, St. Catharines, and I. J. Birchard, M.A., Ph. D., Mathematical Master, Jameson Avenue Collegiate Institute, Toronto. Second edition. 352 pp. Toronto: William Briggs. 1896. 75. 32.

ROBINSON.—The True Sphere of the Blind. By E. B. F. Robinson, B.A., Philosophy Prizeman of Trinity University in 1893. 254 pp. Toronto: Printed for the author by William Briggs. 1896. 1.00. 29.

Contains portrait and illustrations.

ROULEAU.—L'Emigration. Ses Principales Causes. C. E. Rouleau. 150 pp. Québec: Léger Brousseau. 1896. 18.

ROY.—Consultations gratuites. Farce en un acte a trois personnages. Par Régis Roy. Suivie du dialogue-bouffe: Le Sourd. 48 pp. Montréal: C. O. Beauchemin & Fils. 25. 19.

ROY.—On Demande un Acteur. Farce en un acte. Par Régis Roy. Suivie du fameux discours de Baptiste Tranchemontagne: " Qu 'est-ce que la politique? " 36 pp. Montréal: C. O. Beauchemin & Fils. 25. 24.
Copyright 1896.

RUSSELL.—The Nova Scotia Reports, Volume XXVII., containing reports of cases argued and determined in the Supreme Court of Nova Scotia. With a table of the names of cases argued, a table of cases cited, and a digest of the principal matters. Reported by Benjamin Russell, M.A., Q.C., and John M. Geldert, Jr., LL.B., Barristers-at-Law. 14+630 pp. Toronto: The Carswell Company, Ltd. 1896. 5.00 in numbers. 49.

SANKEY.—Sacred Songs, No. 1. Compiled and arranged for use in gospel meetings, Sunday schools, prayer meetings and other religious services. By Ira D. Sankey, James McGranahan and Geo. C. Stebbins. 208 pp. The Copp, Clark Company, Limited. 35. 41.
Copyright 1896.

[SAUNDERS (W. E.).]—Twenty-Sixth Annual Report of the Entomological Society of Ontario, 1895. Published by the Ontario Department of Agriculture, Toronto. Printed by the order of the Legislative Assembly. 4+102 pp. Toronto: Warwick Bros. & Rutter. 1896. 70.
Contains portraits and illustrations.

SHARP.—Consolidated Supplement No. 1. to Sharp's Civil Code. Containing all statutory enactments and a digest of all reported cases affecting the civil code of Lower Canada, from the 1st October, 1888, to 14th October, 1895. By William Prescott Sharp, B.C.L., Advocate. 10+704 pp. Montreal: C. Theoret. 1896. 9.00. 65.

SIMS.—Remarkable Narratives, or, Records of Powerful Revivals, striking providences, wonderful religious experiences, tragic death-bed scenes, and other authentic incidents, to which is added some valuable hints for Christian workers. By Rev. A. Sims. 352 pp. Published and for sale by the Author. Kingston, Ont., Canada. 1896. 1.00. 28.

SMILY.—Canadian Summer Resort Guide. Illustrated souvenir and guide book of some of the principal resorts and tourist and excursion routes of Canada. With maps, and tables of railway and steamboat fares and connections, hotel rates, etc. Third edition.

Edited and published by Frederick Smily, Toronto. 88 pp. Toronto:
Murray Printing Company. 1896. 25. 57.
Contains numerous illustrations. Paper cover.

SMITH.—A Lover in Homespun, and other stories. By F. Clifford
Smith. Second edition. 202 pp. Toronto: William Briggs. 1896.
1.00. 37.

SMITH.—The Ontario Digest 1891-1895 of the cases reported in
volumes 18-22 Appeal Reports. 20-26 Ontario Reports. 14-16
Practice Reports. 18-24 Supreme Court of Canada Reports. 1-3
Exchequer Court of Canada Reports, and of the Canadian cases
decided by the judicial committee of the Privy Council reported in
[1891-1895] appeal cases, with tables of cases contained in the digest,
those affirmed, reversed, or specially considered, and of statutes referred to. Compiled by order of the Law Society of Upper Canada.
By J. F. Smith, Q.C., E. B. Brown, and R. S. Cassels, Barristers-at-
Law. 98+528 pp. Toronto: Rowsell & Hutchison. 1896. Half
calf. 5.00. 64.
Addendum and errata slip inserted in front of title page.

SMITH.—The Ontario Reports. Volume 27. Containing Reports
of Cases decided in the Queen's Bench, Chancery, and Common Pleas
Divisions of the High Court of Justice for Ontario. With a table of
the names of cases argued, a table of the names of cases cited, and a
digest of the principal matters. Editor, James F. Smith, Q.C. Re-
porters: G. F. Harman, A. H. F. Lefroy, G. A. Boomer, E. B. Brown,
Barristers-at-Law. 32+762 pp. Toronto: Rowsell & Hutchison.
1896. Half calf. 5.00. 56.

SMITH.—Mabel Gray, and other poems. By Lyman C. Smith.
132 pp. Toronto: William Briggs. 1896. 1.00. 25.

SNOW.—The Law of Landlord and Tenant in the Province of
Quebec. (Exclusive of Farm Leases.) By F. Longueville Snow.
Editor Monthly Law Digest and Reporter. 12+138, 152-170 pp.
Published by the Author. Printed by John Lovell & Son. 1.75. 50.
Copyright 1896.

[SOUTHWORTH (THOMAS).]—Annual Report of the Clerk of
Forestry for the Province of Ontario, 1896. Printed by order of the
Legislative Assembly. 2+132 pp. Toronto: Warwick Bros. & Rutter.
1896. 70.
Contains illustrations and map. Paper cover.

SOUVENIR.—A Souvenir of the Intercolonial Railway, the popu-
lar and scenic route of Canada. 86 pp. Ottawa: Government Printing Bureau. 1896. 1.
Contains folding map and numerous illustrations. Paper cover.

SPARROW.—The Lady of Chateau Blanc. An Historical Romance. By Malcolm W. Sparrow. 8+70 pp. Toronto: The Brough Printing Co. 1896. 75.

SPEECH.—Speech of the Hon. R. Harcourt, Treasurer of the Province of Ontario, delivered on the nineteenth day of February, 1896, in the Legislative Assembly of the Province of Ontario, on moving the House into committee of supply. 46 pp. Toronto: Warwick Bros. & Rutter. 1896. 50.
Paper cover.

SPENCE.—The Facts of the Case: A summary of the most important evidence and argument presented in the report of the Royal Commission on the Liquor Traffic. Compiled under the direction of the Dominion Alliance for the total suppression of the liquor traffic. By F. S. Spence, Secretary. 336 pp. Toronto: Newton & Treloar. 1896. 25.
With compliments of The Dominion Alliance.

SPENDLOVE.—The Nature of Disease. By F. M. R. Spendlove, M.D. Illustrated. 32 pp. Montreal: "Witness" Printing House. 1896. 10. 19.
Series No. 1. Part I. Paper cover.

STALKER.—The Life of Jesus Christ. By James Stalker, D.D. New and revised edition. 156 pp. Fleming H. Revell Company. New York. Chicago. Toronto. 50. 28.
Copyright 1896. Hand-book for Bible classes.

STALKER.—The Life of St. Paul. By James Stalker, D.D. Glasgow. 6,12-149 pp. Fleming H. Revell Company. New York. Chicago. Toronto. 50. 28.
Copyright 1896. Hand-book for Bible classes.

STATUTES.—Statutes of the Province of British Columbia, passed in the session held in the fifty-ninth year of the reign of Her Majesty Queen Victoria, being the second session of the seventh parliament of British Columbia, begun and holden at Victoria on the 23rd January, and ending on the 17th April, 1896. His Honour the Honourable E. Dewdney, Lieutenant-Governor. 6+532 pp. Victoria, B.C.: Printed by Richard Wolfenden. 1896. 2.50. 75.

STATUTES.—Statutes of the Province of Ontario passed in the session held in the fifty-ninth year of the reign of Her Majesty Queen Victoria, being the second session of the eighth legislature of Ontario, begun and holden at Toronto, on the eleventh day of February in the year of our Lord one thousand eight hundred and ninety-six. His Honour the Honourable George Airey Kirkpatrick, Lieutenant-Governor. 8+658 pp. Toronto: Printed by L. K. Cameron. 1896. 1.50. 64.

3

STATUTES.—The Statutes of Nova Scotia, passed in the fifty-ninth year of the reign of Her Majesty Queen Victoria, being the second session of the thirty-first General Assembly convened in the said Province. 10+306+16 pp. Halifax, N.S.: Commissioner of Public Works and Mines, Queen's Printer. 1896. 1.25. 50.

STEVENSON.—Questions based on Public School History of England and Canada. By R. B. Stevenson, Baldoon, Ont. 72 pp. 15. 8.
Copyright applied ior.

STEVENSON.—Questions based on Public School Physiology and Temperance, with the meaning of the principal terms. By R. B. Stevenson, Baldoon, Ont. 80 pp. 15. 8.

STILLWELL.—Dress, Pride and Beauty. A plea for plainness and naturalness. By Rev. Reuben Stillwell. 16 pp. Toronto: William Briggs. 1896. 5. 29.

STOCK.—The Stock Investors' Handy Pocket Book of Rates. By a Bank Accountant. 52 pp. Toronto: Hart & Riddell. 1896. 50. 8.
Copyright 1885. Printed on one side of the leaf only.

SUMMER.—Summer Tours by the Canadian Pacific Railway. Fishing and shooting grounds. Eastern tours. Western tours. Miscellaneous tours. Tours to the Orient, the Tropics, the Antipodes and around the world. Tenth edition. 200 pp. Issued by Passenger Traffic Department, Canadian Pacific Railway. Montreal. 1896. 54.
Contains maps and numerous illustrations.

SUPPLEMENT.—Supplément a l'Antiphonaire. 603-649, 10 pp. Montréal: C. O. Beauchemin & Fils. 1896. 40. 59.
Paper cover. No title page.

SUPPLEMENT.—Supplément au Graduel. 503-551, 10 pp. Montréal: C. O. Beauchemin & Fils. 1896. 40. 59.
Paper cover. No title page.

SWAN.—A Stormy Voyager. By Annie S. Swan. (Mrs. Burnett-Smith.) With illustrations by R. H. Mather. 6+346 pp. Toronto, Canada: William Briggs. 1.25. 33.
Copyright 1896.

SWAN.—Memories of Margaret Grainger, Schoolmistress. By Annie S. Swan (Mrs. Burnett-Smith). With twelve full-page illustrations by D. Murray Smith. 8×294 pp. Toronto, Canada: William Briggs. 1.00. 33.
Copyright 1896.

TENNYSON.—The Land of Napioa and other Essays in Prose and Verse. By Bertram Tennyson, Q.C. 14+164 pp. The Spectator Printing and Publishing Co., Moosomin, N.W.T. 30. 18.
Copyright 1896. Paper cover.

TETU.—Histoire du Palais Episcopal de Québec. Par Mgr. Henri Têtu, Prélat de la Maison de sa Sainteté. 304 pp. Québec: Librairie Montmorency-Laval. Pruneau & Kirouac. 1896. 50.
Contains views, plans and portraits.

THOMAS.—History of the Counties of Argenteuil, Que., and Prescott, Ont., from the Earliest Settlement to the Present. By C. Thomas. 666 pp. Montreal: Printed by John Lovell & Son. 1896. 2.50. 65.
Contains portraits and other illustrations

THOMPSON.—Leasehold Arbitrations. How the system of renewal and awards results in practical confiscation. By Phillips Thompson. 24 pp. Toronto: James & Williams. 1896. 25. 57.

THOMSON.—Walter Gibbs, the Young Boss, and other stories. A book for boys. By Edward William Thomson. 6+362 pp. Toronto: William Briggs. 1.25. 32.
Copyright 1896. Contains several plates.

TORONTO.—The Toronto City Directory, 1896. Vol. 20. Embracing an alphabetical list of all business firms and private citizens; a classified business directory; a miscellaneous directory—containing a large amount of valuable information, and a complete street guide. Also suburban directories of Bedford Park, Bracondale, Chester, Coleman, Davisville, Deer Park, Doncaster, East Toronto, Eglinton, Humber Bay, Lambton Mills, Little York, Mimico, New Toronto, North Dovercourt, North Toronto, Norway, Swansea, Todmorden, Toronto Junction and Wychwood Park. 51-1756 pp. Compiled and published by the Might Directory Company of Toronto, Ltd.: Toronto, Ont. 1896. 6.00. 59.

TORONTO.—Toronto Public Library. Catalogue of the Books in the Circulating Library. Vol. 2. Central Public Library, corner Church and Adelaide streets. 8+316 pp. 1896. 50. 57.

TRANSACTIONS.—Transactions of the Astronomical and Physical Society of Toronto, for the year 1895, including sixth annual report. 10+182+6 pp. Toronto: Rowsell & Hutchison. 1896. 1.00. 46.
Paper cover. Contains illustrations.

TRUDELLE.—Charlesbourg. Mélanges historiographiques, aussi La Légende d'un Tableau hors texte. Par Joseph Trudelle, de la bibliothèque de la Législature de la Province de Québec. 8+256 pp. Québec: Frs. N. Faveur. 1896. 13.

UNIVERSITIES.—The Universities of Canada. Their history and organization. With an outline of British and American University Systems. Appendix to the report of the Minister of Education, 1896. 8+440 pp. Toronto: Printed by Warwick Bros. & Rutter. 1896. 28.

[WADE (HENRY).]—Fiftieth Annual Report of the Agriculture and Arts Association of Ontario, 1895. Printed by order of the Legislative Assembly. 4+192 pp. Toronto: Warwick Bros. & Rutter. 1896. 70.

WALKER.—An Itinerant in the British Isles. By Rev. W. W. Walker. 206 pp. Toronto: William Briggs. 1896. 75. 28.
Contains numerous illustrations.

WALKER.—By Northern Lakes. Reminiscences of Life in Ontario Mission Fields. By Rev. W. W. Walker. Illustrated. 168 pp. Toronto: William Briggs. 1896. 75. 29.

WALLACE.—Speech of Hon. N. Clarke Wallace, M.P., on the Remedial Bill, Ottawa, Tuesday, 3rd March, 1896. House of Commons Debates. Sixth session, seventh Parliament. 8 pp. 65.

[WATSON (JOHN).]—Kate Carnegie and Those Ministers. By Ian Maclaren. 10+358 pp. Toronto: Fleming H. Revell Company. 1896. 1.25. 29.

WATSON.—The Cure of Souls. Lyman Beecher. Lectures on Preaching at Yale University. 1896. By John Watson, M.A., D.D. 10+302 pp. Toronto: Fleming H. Revell Company. 1.25. 29.
Copyright 1896.

WATSON.—The Mind of the Master. By John Watson, D.D. (Ian Maclaren.) 8+338 pp. Toronto: Fleming H. Revell Company. 1.25. 29.
Copyright 1896.

WETHERELL.—Later American Poems. Edited by J. E. Wetherell, B.A. 16+256 pp. Toronto: The Copp, Clark Company, Limited. 1896. Paper. 35. Cloth. 50. 17.
Contains numerous portraits.

WILLSON.—The Municipal Act. Consolidated, Condensed, Classified. Text book for the Municipal Law School, Toronto. By Arthur L. Willson, B.A., Toronto, Ont. 8+132 pp. Toronto: Printed by the Carswell Co., Ltd. 1896. 1.00. 56.

WILSON.—Rays of Light from Bible Lands: embracing historical sketches of The Five Great Empires of Antiquity, Egypt, Nineveh, Babylon, Tyre and Persia, whose remarkable career and complete overthrow attest to the truths of sacred story. By Rev. Robert Wilson, Ph.D. Also a graphic description of the Harvest Home in Palestine; or, Israel's national thanksgiving festival and its signification. By A. L. O. N. B. Together with a connected record of Rev. Dr. Talmage's tour to, through, and from the Holy Land. The whole forming a treasury of valuable information designed to assist the

Bible reader to a better understanding of the Scriptures. 88+32 pp.
St. John, N.B.: R. A. H. Morrow. 1896. 50. 37.

Contains several illustrations.

WINTER.—The Complete Church Choir Record. Containing
(minutes) of business meetings, record of attendance of members,
record of music rendered at church services, programmes of concerts,
or song services given, record of cash received and paid out. In one
book. Including also a short chapter each on "Hints to Choirs,"
and "Duties of Officers and Members." 144 pp. Prepared and published by Charles A. Winter, Organizer and Secretary of the annual
gathering of the united choirs of Western Ontario. Preston, Ont.
(Late of Waterloo). 1.00. 79.

Copyright 1896.

WINTLE.—The Birds of Montreal. By Ernest D. Wintle, " As-
sociate Member of the American Ornithologists' Union." Birds ob-
served in the vicinity of Montreal, Province of Quebec, Dominion of
Canada, with annotations as to whether they are "Permanent Residents" or those that are found regularly throughout the year;
"Winter Visitants," or those that occur only during the winter sea-
son, passing north in the spring; "Transient Visitants," or those that
occur only during migrations in spring and autumn; "Summer
Residents," or those that are known to breed, but which depart south-
ward before winter; and "Accidental Visitants," or stragglers from
remote districts; giving their relative abundance as to whether they
are rare, scarce, common or abundant; data of nests and eggs when
found, and especially noting the species that breed in the City and
Mount Royal Park; also data of migratory arrivals and departures,
and other notes, all of which are deduced from original observations
made during the past fifteen years. 14+282 pp. Montreal: W. Drysdale & Co. 1896. 1.25. 51.

Contains map and two plates. Includes original sporting sketches compiled by David Denne, 1895. Frontispiece and two plates. Fish and Game
Laws, 1896.

WOODS.—Harrison Hall and its Associations, or a History of the
Municipal, Judicial, and Educational Interests of the Western Penin-
sula. By R. S. Woods, Q.C., Junior Judge of Kent. 152 pp. Chatham Planet Book and Job Dept. 1896. 1.00 55.

Contains portrait and view.

[WOOLVERTON (L.).]—Second Annual Report of the Fruit
Experiment Stations of Ontario, under the joint control of the Ontario Agricultural College, Guelph, and the Fruit Growers' Association of Ontario. 1895. (Published by the Ontario Department of
Agriculture, Toronto.) Printed by order of the Legislative Assembly.
124 pp. Toronto: Warwick Bros. & Rutter. 1896. 70.

Contains numerous illustrations.

[WOOLVERTON (L.).]—Twenty-Seventh Annual Report of the Fruit Growers' Association of Ontario, 1895. (Published by the Ontario Department of Agriculture, Toronto.) Printed by order of the Legislative Assembly. 4+128 pp. Toronto: Warwick Bros. & Rutter. 1896. 70.

WORTH.—Worth's Burlesque Ritual, includes initiation of a candidate, opening and closing ceremony, minutes, orders of business, etc., with general instructions, written for the purpose of creating amusement at anniversaries of secret societies and for public entertainments, material for over two hours' solid fun. By Edward Worth, Kent Bridge, Ontario. 20 pp. 6 for 5.00. 28.

Copyright 1896.

TITLE INDEX.

INDEX TABLE OF SIZES.

Sizes in inches, with numbers to correspond.

No.	Size	No.	Size	No.	Size
1	4¾ x 6½	29	7½ x 5	57	8¾ x 6
2	4¾ x 7	30	7¼ x 5¼	58	9 x 5¾
3	5¼ x 3½	31	7¼ x 6	59	9 x 6
4	5¼ x 2¾	32	7½ x 5	60	9¼ x 6
5	5½ x 4	33	7½ x 5¼	61	9¼ x 6¼
6	5¾ x 2¾	34	7½ x 5½	62	9¼ x 6½
7	5¾ x 4	35	7½ x 5¾	63	9¼ x 7½
8	5¾ x 4¼	36	7¾ x 4¾	64	9¼ x 6½
9	5¾ x 4½	37	7¾ x 5¼	65	9¼ x 6½
10	6 x 3¾	38	7¾ x 5½	66	9¼ x 6¾
11	6 x 4	39	7¾ x 5¾	67	9½ x 7¼
12	6¼ x 4	40	7¾ x 9	68	9½ x 7¼
13	6¼ x 4¼	41	8 x 5¼	69	9¾ x 6½
14	6¼ x 4½	42	8 x 5½	70	9¾ x 6¼
15	6½ x 4½	43	8 x 5¾	71	9¾ x 6¾
16	6½ x 4¾	44	8¼ x 5	72	9¾ x 7½
17	6½ x 5	45	8¼ x 5¼	73	10 x 6½
18	6¾ x 4¼	46	8¼ x 5½	74	10 x 6¾
19	6¾ x 4½	47	8¼ x 6	75	10 x 7
20	6¾ x 4¾	48	8½ x 5	76	10 x 7½
21	6¾ x 5	49	8½ x 5½	77	10½ x 7½
22	6¾ x 5¼	50	8½ x 5¾	78	10½ x 7½
23	7 x 4½	51	8½ x 6	79	10½ x 6½
24	7 x 4½	52	8½ x 6¾	80	12½ x 9¼
25	7 x 4¾	53	8½ x 7½	81	13 x 8½
26	7 x 5	54	8¾ x 4½	82	5¼ x 3¾
27	7¼ x 4½	55	8¾ x 5½	83	8 x 4¾
28	7¼ x 4¾	56	8¾ x 5¾		

PUBLICATIONS OF HAIGHT & CO.,

TORONTO, ONTARIO, CANADA,

ANNUAL CANADIAN CATALOGUE OF BOOKS. 1896. By W. R. Haight. First Supplement to the Canadian Catalogue of Books (1791-1895). 60 pp. Demy 8vo, paper uncut. Toronto: 1898. Edition 500 copies............................ $2 00

BEFORE THE COMING OF THE LOYALISTS. U. E. Series. No. 1. By C. Haight, author of " Country Life in Canada Fifty Years Ago "; " Here and There in the Home Land." 24 pp. Demy 8vo, paper uncut. Toronto: 1897. Edition 1000 copies.. 25

CANADIAN CATALOGUE OF BOOKS. Part I. (1791-1895). By W. R. Haight. 10 + 132 pp. Demy 8vo, paper uncut. Toronto: 1896. Edition 509 copies........................... 2 50

"'The Canadian Catalogue of Books,' Part I., has been issued by W. R. Haight, Toronto. It really fills 'a long-felt want,' and is a first instalment of what booksellers have been looking for—a catalogue of all Canadian editions."— *Canada Bookseller and Stationer, Toronto, February, 1897.*

" The publications recorded make up an interesting and heterogeneous collection ranging from the relations of the Jesuit Fathers to government reports, surveys, sermons, society pamphlets, privately-printed poems, Canadian editions of well-known books, and standard works in the various fields of literature. It will be seen that the work as it now stands is far from being a complete catologue of Canadian books; indeed, this is expressly disclaimed in the preface. It is, however, a beginning toward a systematic Canadian trade bibliography, and as such deserves a cordial welcome."—*The Publishers' Weekly, October 24th, 1896.*

www.ingramcontent.com/pod-product-compliance
Lightning Source LLC
Chambersburg PA
CBHW030720110426
42739CB00030B/1039